A-LEVEL YEAR 2

STUDENT GUIDE

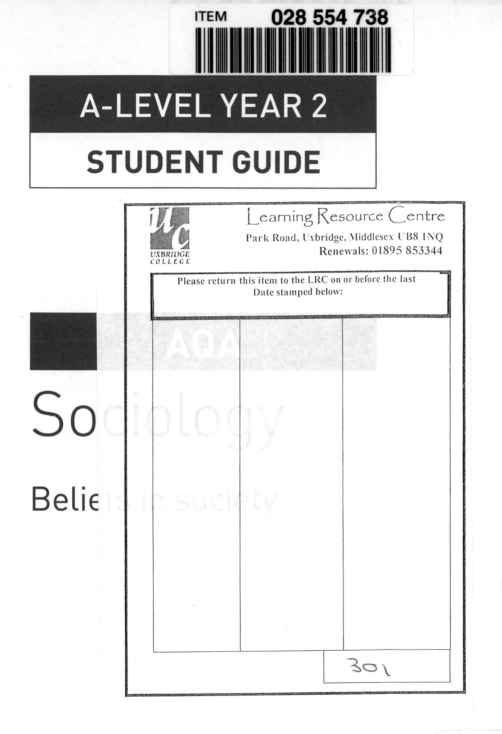

AQA

Sociology

Beliefs in society

Joan Garrod

HODDER
EDUCATION
AN HACHETTE UK COMPANY

Acknowledgement: With grateful thanks to Tony Lawson.

Hodder Education, an Hachette UK company, Blenheim Court, George Street, Banbury, Oxfordshire OX16 5BH

Orders

Bookpoint Ltd, 130 Park Drive, Milton Park, Abingdon, Oxfordshire OX14 4SB

tel: 01235 827827

fax: 01235 400401

e-mail: education@bookpoint.co.uk

Lines are open 9.00 a.m.–5.00 p.m., Monday to Saturday, with a 24-hour message answering service. You can also order through the Hodder Education website: www.hoddereducation. co.uk

© Joan Garrod 2016

ISBN 978-1-4718-5774-4

First printed 2016

Impression number 5 4 3 2 1

Year 2020 2019 2018 2017 2016

This Guide has been written specifically to support students preparing for the AQA A-level Sociology examinations. The content has been neither approved nor endorsed by AQA and remains the sole responsibility of the author.

Cover photo: Marco Govel/Fotolia

Typeset by Integra Software Services Pvt. Ltd., Pondicherry, India

Printed in Italy

Hachette UK's policy is to use papers that are natural, renewable and recyclable products and made from wood grown in sustainable forests. The logging and manufacturing processes are expected to conform to the environmental regulations of the country of origin.

Contents

Content Guidance

Questions & Answers

■ Getting the most from this book

Exam tips

Advice on key points in the text to help you learn and recall content, avoid pitfalls, and polish your exam technique in order to boost your grade.

Knowledge check

Rapid-fire questions throughout the Content Guidance section to check your understanding.

Knowledge check answers

1 Turn to the back of the book for the Knowledge check answers.

Summaries

■ Each core topic is rounded off by a bullet-list summary for quick-check reference of what you need to know.

Exam-style questions

Commentary on the questions

Tips on what you need to do to gain full marks, indicated by the icon ⓔ

Sample student answers

Practise the questions, then look at the student answers that follow.

Questions & Answers

15 Read Item B below and answer the question that follows.

Item B
The regular worshippers at most Christian churches are increasingly female. Since the Church of England voted to permit the ordination of women, and now has a female bishop, many women have expressed an interest in becoming ministers, and there are now more women than men in training for the ministry. It has been argued that the greater participation of women in many aspects of religious life has led to religion becoming 'gendered', which partly explains the growing absence of men at religious services.

Applying material from Item B and your own knowledge, evaluate the view that religion is becoming increasingly feminised.   [20 marks]

ⓔ This question gives you ample opportunity to show your knowledge of gender in different religious groups and faiths.

Student A

13 Secularisation refers to the declining importance of religion both for individuals and for society, and the proportion of people attending religious services is used as one indicator of this.

ⓔ While not essential, this type of brief introduction showing a clear understanding of the concept and the question is always helpful — though it does need to be brief.

The question talks about 'church attendance statistics', which is obviously a reference to the Christian religion. As a way of measuring the extent of secularisation, it is obviously not sufficient. The recent important report into Religion in Public Life emphasised many times that Britain is now a multi-faith society. Being able to show that attendance at Sunday worship for Christians is falling — which it is — is therefore showing only part of the picture.

ⓔ A relevant point, clearly expressed and with reference to an important report.

Islam, Hinduism, Judaism and Sikhism are also important faiths in Britain (in terms of numbers) so we would have to look at the picture in these faiths before being able to make statements about the extent of secularisation. This might prove problematic in that attendance statistics are not gathered in the same way for all faiths. It is difficult to find statistics for attendance at mosques in Britain, though evidence from Spain indicates that the longer a Muslim immigrant lives in a European country, the less likely s/he is to go regularly to a mosque. In addition to other major religions, some people are members of NRMs or New Age groups, for which few statistics are available, and many groups do not have any kind of formal act of worship, though their members might be religious — or at least have spiritual beliefs. So, using only Christian church attendance statistics is problematic when judging the extent of secularisation.

Commentary on sample student answers

Read the comments (preceded by the icon ⓔ) showing how many marks each answer would be awarded in the exam and exactly where marks are gained or lost.

■About this book

This guide covers the topic of *Beliefs in society* in the AQA A-level specification 7192. Remember that this is a guide, not a textbook. It indicates and briefly explains and discusses those things that you should know and understand about this topic, but is intended to complement, not replace, your textbooks and class notes.

How to use this guide

The first main section of the book is **Content Guidance**. It follows the headings for this topic and the sequence in which they occur in the AQA specification, but it is not necessary to read them in this order, provided you make sure that you cover them all.

In your study of this topic area you should examine the two **core themes**. These are:
- socialisation, culture and identity
- social differentiation, power and stratification.

These are not things to be studied separately — rather, in your study of *Beliefs in society* you should be aware of the two core themes running through the topic.

You should also be aware of both the **evidence** for and the **sociological explanations** of the content of this topic. This means that you must study the relevant sociological theories, perspectives and methods associated with this topic, as well as the design of the research used to obtain any data under consideration, including its strengths and limitations.

Each section of the Content Guidance contains exam tips, knowledge checks and definitions of some key terms. Knowing and understanding the meaning of sociological concepts is an essential part of the whole course.

The second main section of the book is that of **Questions & Answers**. At the beginning of this section are the three assessment objectives against which your exam answers will be judged, with some guidance regarding how to display the required skills, and also a list of command words, which will help you to understand more clearly what each question is asking you to do. The five test papers provided are in the style of the AQA exam for this topic. More detailed guidance on how to use the Questions & Answers section is given at the beginning of that section.

Content Guidance

■ Ideology, science and religion

Ideology

An ideology is a set of ideas and beliefs held by an individual, group or society which reflects their needs or aspirations and which is used to make sense of their world. Many important ideologies are political and/or economic, such as Marxism or conservatism, but ideologies are also found in religious beliefs, such as Islam or Catholicism. Ideologies are used to guide or inform people's behaviour.

Science

The term 'science' refers both to a method of enquiry and to a particular body of knowledge, such as chemistry or physics. The scientific method of enquiry aims to discover regularities and recurring relationships between variables by a rigorous system of observation, conjecture, **hypothesis** formation and controlled testing, with the object of identifying theories (confirmed hypotheses) and eventually scientific laws. The goal is to understand the natural world in order to make predictions and, where possible, to control it.

Some see religion and science as incompatible with each other, and there are examples of conflict, for example between those whose religious beliefs encompass the idea of creationism (that the Bible story of God creating the world in six days is literally true) and the scientific beliefs and evidence regarding evolution. However, research suggests that almost a half of scientists hold some religious beliefs and see no problem with this. Albert Einstein, writing in *The New York Times Magazine* on 9 November 1930, said: 'I maintain that the cosmic religious feeling is the strongest and noblest motive for scientific research.' Many scientists and religious believers take the position that science tries to discover the 'how', while religious belief explores the 'why'. Einstein also wrote: 'Science without religion is lame; religion without science is blind.' These views would not, however, be accepted by Richard Dawkins, an evolutionary biologist and atheist, who is very outspoken in his views and who holds that religion is incompatible with science.

One of the first major conflicts between the Christian church and science occurred in the sixteenth and seventeenth centuries, when Copernicus and Galileo claimed that the sun was at the centre of the universe, and that the earth and other planets moved around it — a view known as heliocentrism. The religious view was that this was **heretical**, as the Bible showed that the Earth was the centre, and books that claimed otherwise were placed on the list of prohibited reading. A more serious scientific challenge to the authority of the church was Darwin's theory of evolution, and this continues to cause controversy today, between those accepting Darwinian theory and creationists, who hold that the Bible stories of the Earth's creation are literally true.

Hypothesis An unverified idea that offers a possible explanation of an observed phenomenon. In short, it can be seen as an untested 'theory'. It provides a direction for the research but needs to be rigorously tested to see whether it continues to explain the phenomenon under investigation. The testing or experiments should show whether the hypothesis is confirmed, refuted or needs to be modified.

Knowledge check 1

By what term is the scientific method of enquiry generally known?

Heretical Views that disagree with or challenge accepted doctrine, especially that of religion.

With the spread of the Enlightenment and scientific views, many former teachings of the church have been changed or dropped, and it is suggested that only the church's core teachings remain intact. Even many church ministers now accept that the Bible stories should be taken **allegorically** rather than literally. The current situation tends to be that the church is the authority on moral and spiritual issues, while science deals with factual matters.

Religion

Broadly speaking, what we term 'religion' refers to a set of ideas and beliefs relating to the supernatural world, dealing with questions such as the meaning of life and death and what happens after death, and which also provides a moral code stating how one should live one's life.

There is no single accepted definition of what we mean by 'religion'. Nevertheless, definitions are important because they are used to decide what should be examined as a religious phenomenon and what should be excluded. The definition adopted will lead sociologists to ask different questions about the nature, scale and importance of religious belief and activity in society, often leading them to different conclusions.

Some of the most important definitions are:

- Inclusivist definitions: these include many phenomena that to some might seem controversial, such as magic, or even non-religious beliefs, such as communism. They are 'essentialist', meaning that they take the position that religious belief and activity are necessary features of the human condition, though they may take many different forms. Giddens (1997) uses an inclusivist definition of religion. He sees religion as having the following characteristics:
  - a set of symbols invoking feelings of reverence or awe
  - a set of rituals or ceremonials engaged in by a community of believers
  - beliefs which do not necessarily involve gods but 'some beings inspiring attitudes of awe or wonder'.
- Exclusivist definitions: these exclude phenomena that make no reference to a supernatural being or beings, and therefore limit what will be defined as religious. They are 'non-essentialist', accepting that religious belief and activity may grow or decline in different historical periods. Stark and Bainbridge (1985) use an exclusivist definition of religion when they argue that religions must involve some conception of a supernatural being, world or force, and the notion that events and conditions on Earth are influenced by the supernatural.
- Substantive definitions: these refer to a defining characteristic, such as a belief in God, as the distinctive feature of a religion.
- Functional definitions: these focus on the role that religion performs for society as a whole, such as acting as a unifying force.

Religions may also be classified according to the number of deities.

- Monotheistic religions are those with a belief in a single god or deity. Examples are Christianity and Islam.
- Polytheistic religions are those with a belief in a panoply, or group, of deities. Examples are the religious beliefs of the Romans, Greeks and Native American

Allegory When a story or picture of everyday things is used to reveal a hidden meaning, often something moral or spiritual.

Knowledge check 2

Give an example of a belief system that would fit into an exclusivist definition of religion.

Knowledge check 3

Which sociological perspective focuses on the alleged unifying aspect of religion?

tribes, and Hinduism. In fact, with the exception of what are considered the major world religions, most religions are polytheistic.

■ Henotheistic religions are those in which the religion has a belief in and worships just one god, but acknowledges the actual or possible existence of other deities.

Knowledge check 4

Give an example of a monotheistic world religion other than Christianity and Islam.

Evaluation

+ Inclusivist-functionalist definitions allow the sociologist to investigate a wide range of historical and contemporary practices as 'religious', including humanism and psychoanalysis, because these are concerned with the 'ultimate problems' that confront all human beings.
+ Exclusivist-substantive definitions allow the sociologist to examine only those social phenomena that are normally recognised as expressions of religious feeling.
+ Both the above approaches are attempting to identify what can be 'religious' in order to form a field of study with definite boundaries.
- Inclusivist-functional definitions are so encompassing that they make the idea of a specifically religious sphere of activity difficult to identify — everything can be seen as 'religious'.
- Exclusivist-substantive definitions limit what can be seen as religious and lead inevitably to the idea that in many societies religious observance has declined in importance.
- Both the above approaches are actually linked to ideological positions that are associated with either supporting or undermining the extent of religious belief.

Exam tip

It is always a good idea to show that you know that 'religion' may be defined in different ways. If it is relevant to your answer, explain which definition(s) you are using.

Key thinkers

Durkheim (1858–1917)

Durkheim started from the position that 'social existence' — people living together in societies — was possible only through shared beliefs.

His was a functionalist definition of religion, which focused on the positive role it played, namely 'beliefs and practices which unite into one single moral community called a Church'. Religion was therefore an essential part of the shared consciousness ('conscience collective') that makes social life possible. The shared consciousness includes ideas about time, space, causation and social relationships.

Durkheim distinguished between 'the profane', which was normal, everyday life, and 'the sacred', which referred to what he called things 'set apart and forbidden'. This meant shared rituals and the worship of objects held to be sacred, such as totems. The origin of these ideas was his study of the totemic religions of the Australian Aborigines, in which the sacred object of the totem represented the clan or tribe. In this way the totem symbolised society, and the collective rituals restated the importance and significance of shared social bonds. Religion thus acted to bind individuals to society, enabling them to understand and accept approved social relationships through the shared values of religious belief. Religion also served to regulate people's behaviour by providing moral guidance, which enabled people to live together in society without the problems caused by selfish individualism.

Knowledge check 5

Give two examples of a shared religious ritual.

Key concepts

'conscience collective'; sacred and profane; shared rituals; moral guidance

Evaluation

+ Religion is given a dominant role in the establishment and maintenance of social cohesion.
+ Social relationships are given a moral dimension, based on shared religious beliefs.
+ The existence of religion is explained in terms of its rituals, rather than its particular theological ideas.
- The importance of individual religious experience is ignored.
- This is a static view of religion — Durkheim did not attempt to explain the rise of new religions or religious leaders.
- The evidence for Durkheim's views was based on the study of very small, atypical societies.
- The practices of primitive religions cannot easily be applied to complex, religiously diverse modern societies.

Marx (1818–83)

For Marx, religion was a human project. 'Man makes religion, religion doesn't make man.' In particular, religion is the product of those in power — those who control the productive process. However, religion is not the product of the bourgeoisie but of historical systems of exploitation — religion existed long before capitalism. Religion cannot be eliminated until the conditions that cause it are eliminated, i.e. exploitation. Marx saw religion as an aspect of ideology which was an important element in the '**false consciousness**' of both the working class and the bourgeoisie, in that neither group had a real appreciation of their position as pawns of the system.

For the members of the working class, religion is both the expression of real distress and the means of alleviating it. Religion blinds them to their true condition, i.e. one of exploitation, and socialises them into a set of beliefs that is contrary to their interests. In particular, it teaches them that obedience to authority ('accepting God's will') is their route to salvation, which will await them in the afterlife.

Religion also presents the bourgeoisie with a 'cloak of respectability' behind which they can continue to make profit out of the exploitation of their workers because this is 'divine will'. However, Marx believed that both the bourgeoisie and the proletariat were subject to the impersonal forces of capitalism, which favoured and destroyed individuals in an apparently random fashion.

'**False consciousness**' A term used by Marx to describe the beliefs, particularly of the proletariat, that did not reflect their actual position (one of exploitation) but came from ruling class ideology. False consciousness prevented members of the working class from seeing their 'true' class position.

Knowledge check 6

Marx wrote that religion is 'the opium of the people'. Briefly explain what is meant by this.

Evaluation

+ Religion is seen as being determined by the economic base (substructure) rather than theological ideas.
+ Christian religious ideas are explained in terms of how they benefit capitalism.
+ There is an acknowledgement that for the proletariat, religion can help to ease the pain of exploitation.
+ The idea that the bourgeoisie are carrying out God's will enables them to continue their pursuit of profit and exploitation of the proletariat.
− The explanation of religion is monocausal, i.e. its sole origin is the economic base of society.
− There is little evidence to show that the working class had ever been particularly religious.
− Marx may have over-stated the role of religion in ruling-class ideology.

Weber (1864–1920)

Weber studied a number of worldwide religions, and conducted extensive studies of Hinduism, Buddhism, Taoism and Judaism. However, he is best known for his 'Protestant ethic thesis' on the rise of Protestantism and its effect on economic behaviour and social change. Weber was interested in exploring the origin of the 'ethics' of capitalism and suggested that these lay in the beliefs of the seventeenth-century Calvinist religious sect. These included a view that worldly work was a 'calling', rather like a religious vocation, and hard work was seen as a way of honouring God. Calvinists also believed in predestination, that from the moment of creation, God had already decided who was to be 'saved'. These decisions could not be changed and could not be known. In order to cope with this uncertainty, Calvinists looked for signs of God's favour in their lives, with economic success seen as a sign of 'election' to the chosen. Emphasis was on a sober, thrifty lifestyle and in the 'stewardship' of wealth and the reinvestment of profit, rather than on displays of conspicuous consumption. It was Weber's argument that this particular set of beliefs, and the consequences that stemmed from it, provided the right social and economic climate for the development of what he called 'modern capitalism'. Weber used these arguments to show that, under certain circumstances, religious beliefs could be instrumental in bringing about social change and that religion was not, as Marx had claimed, necessarily a conservative force in society.

Primarily, Weber was interested in the meanings which individual social actors imposed on social action in order to make sense of the world. This reflects Weber's interpretative approach to sociology and the importance of 'verstehen'.

Elective affinity
As used by Weber, the term refers to the relationship between beliefs, the actions that follow from those beliefs, and the unintended consequences of those actions.

Verstehen
Understanding social life by uncovering the meanings people ascribe to their actions.

Key concepts
Protestant ethic; Calvinism; predestination; social change; verstehen

Evaluation
+ Weber stressed the importance of individual beliefs as factors in social developments, rejecting economic determinism.
+ Social change is seen as a complex interplay of forces, but there are decisive points in history that can be uncovered by sociological analysis.
+ This is a cross-cultural approach to social change, using data from different societies to explore a hypothesis and come to a conclusion.
− Weber did not demonstrate how strongly individual entrepreneurs held their religious beliefs and therefore the extent to which these may have influenced their behaviour.
− A study of the origins of Calvinism has shown that modern capitalism was already in existence at that time.
− It has been argued that it was not the religious beliefs of the Calvinists but their marginal position in Catholic society that led them to strive for wealth.

Key theories of religion

Functionalism and neo-functionalism

Though drawn from Durkheim, functionalist thought on religion differs from his views in certain critical respects. Totemism is not a set of unified practices but covers a wide range of beliefs and activities. Levi-Strauss believed that totemism can be seen not as the individual's relationship to the social group but as an expression of the relationship between the individual and the natural world.

Malinowski saw religion as the response of individuals to the uncertainty of the world, providing them with a sense of security. However, he did not view religion as an expression of the worship of society.

Functionalist views on religion began to be challenged, particularly from the mid-twentieth century onwards, by the apparent rise of secularisation (see p. 35) and the decline of the Christian church in many Western countries.

Parsons agreed with Durkheim that the shared moral values arising from religious beliefs help to maintain a stable society. He saw religion as continuing to fulfil some of the 'needs' of society. Bellah also believed that religion continues to perform essential social functions. He argued that a process of 'individuation' had taken place, meaning that people increasingly sought religious meanings on an individual basis, rather than through a collective entity such as a church. O'Dea also believed that the function of religion is to provide answers to fundamental questions about life, death and suffering.

Exam tip

Make sure that you can distinguish between the views of Durkheim and those of other functionalist writers on religion. You could bring in more general criticisms of functionalism, such as taking something that exists in society and deciding that it must therefore have a positive function.

Bellah introduced the concept of 'civil religion', by which he meant the adoption of religious ideas, rituals and symbols to bind society together. His ideas were developed with regard to American society, though they are now applied more widely. Some examples would be pledging allegiance to the flag and US presidents ending their speeches with the words 'God bless America'. Others have suggested that Armistice Day commemorations, coronations and the response to the death of Diana, Princess of Wales are also examples of 'civil religions'.

Key concepts

social integration; the supernatural; 'needs' of society; functions, civil religion

Evaluation

+ Recognises the positive role of religion in providing a moral code and in helping individuals though times of emotional crisis, e.g. the death of a family member.
+ Looks at the social dimensions of religion rather than simply individual experiences, in particular tries to explain how individuals can live together in society.
+ Deals with the supernatural as a 'real' phenomenon of subjective experience.
- Asserts rather than explains how religion reinforces common values, especially in multi-religious societies.
- Doesn't acknowledge that religious participation can exist without sincere religious belief.
- Ignores the dysfunctional aspects of religion, e.g. religious conflict within a society.
- Has an undue emphasis on the role of religion as a conservative force in society.

Knowledge check 8
Give an example of an important religious symbol associated with (a) Christianity, (b) Islam and (c) Judaism.

Neo-Marxism

Neo-Marxist writers have taken a less deterministic view of religion than Marx and acknowledged that religious ideas could sometimes act as a force for social change to benefit the working class, as in the case of liberation theology (see p. 17). Gramsci (1971) used the concept of **hegemony** to show how some of society's institutions, including religion, can shape people's beliefs and perceptions of the world. However, it is almost impossible to maintain complete hegemonic control, so there is always the possibility that the dominant ideas of the ruling class could be challenged. Maduro (1982) also believes that the role of religion is more complex than Marx suggested, and that at certain periods religion can be relatively autonomous rather than always supporting and preserving the status quo. Turner (1983) suggests that religious beliefs can sometimes be used to unify the ruling class rather than act to justify the oppression of the working class, which he believes was the case in feudal Britain.

Hegemony In this context, refers to the situation in which a dominant group controls subservient groups not by force but by particular ideas. Thus, persuading the working class that an unequal society is both normal and can be justified by religious beliefs allows members of the bourgeoisie to rule without the constant threat of revolution.

> **Evaluation**
>
> + Acknowledges that religion can sometimes act independently of the substructure.
> + Shows how religion can sometimes benefit the working class.
> + Accepts that the ruling class cannot always achieve complete hegemonic control.
> − Can overstate the revolutionary aspects of religion — in most cases, it is used to support the status quo and helps to preserve the power of the ruling class.

Interactionism

Interactionism looks at the micro aspects of religion, i.e. how it relates to individuals and individual experiences. In other words, it looks at what religion does for the individual.

Interactionists take an inclusive view of religion. The focus on the individual means that they include as 'religious' some things that others would not. Their definition is therefore 'nominal' — they have no set idea of what should constitute a religion.

Like Marx, interactionists see 'cosmologies' (ideas about the world and our place within it) as social constructs, developed and maintained by individual beliefs. Luckmann sees religion as helping to develop a sense of 'self' — of who we are and of our place within the world. In the past, this was acquired through traditional religion, but is now more likely to stem from ideas such as self-expression and self-realisation. Luckmann refers to this as 'invisible religion'.

Again like Marx, interactionists see religion as a form of ideology, but rather than expressing the power of one class over another, the ideology of religion provides a framework for interpreting and understanding the world. Religion gives us categories and concepts that help us to make sense of the world and helps to provide answers to the existential questions of life, death, joy and suffering.

Interactionism focuses on the meaning that individuals give to things. Ideas and practices are not sacred unless and until people believe them to be, and only then do they take on special significance and bring meaning to our lives.

Objects and symbols are imbued with power and provide meanings that are opposed to the chaos that confronts individuals as they try to make sense of their life. Some people and objects are cloaked by the '**sacred canopy**', which gives them special power and meanings.

Interactionists look at how people use religious symbols and imbue them with deep religious significance.

Because of its focus on the individual, interactionism acknowledges that people are free to choose or change their religious beliefs and practices according to their needs and inclinations — what some have called the 'pick and mix' view of religion.

> **Exam tip**
>
> Make quite sure that you can explain what is meant by 'religion as a form of ideology', as it applies to more than one sociological perspective.

> **Knowledge check 9**
>
> Give an example of a person holding office in the Roman Catholic Church who would be described as being cloaked by the 'sacred canopy'.

Sacred canopy A term used by Berger to describe the way in which religious beliefs provide an overarching system of meaning to help people understand and explain the world.

> **Exam tip**
>
> It is a good idea with 'theories of religion' to make a list showing those areas where different theories agree with one or more others.

Key concepts

cosmologies; invisible religion; religious symbols; sacred canopy

Evaluation

+ Religion is seen as having real meaning for people and not as 'false consciousness'.
+ It is seen as still having a positive function even in the context of growing secularisation.
+ Religion is seen as a social construct but one that provides a framework of meaning to help make sense of the world.
- Places too great an emphasis on subjective meanings, as well as assuming that there is a common culture.
- Assumes that religion is a universal human need, despite some people leading fulfilling lives without religion.
- Fails to examine the conflict that occurs within and between religious faiths.

Postmodernism

A key feature of postmodernism is the belief in the end of 'metanarratives', the so-called 'big ideas' of science and rationality regarding how society is structured and organised. Some of these ideas are relevant to religious beliefs and practices. The range of sociologists' responses to ideas of postmodernism is very wide — there is no single agreed position. However, many see religion as a source of reassurance and moral guidance in societies increasingly characterised by insecurities brought about by the loosening of kinship and community ties and the increase in individual freedom and choice.

Bauman links postmodernity to the decline of certainty, authority and objectivity, and the rise of 'neo-tribalism'. This refers to new ways of 'belonging' to groups, based on often temporary shared interests rather than the traditional links of kinship, community and religion.

Giddens develops the concept of 'disembedding' to refer to the ways in which cultural practices and social relationships are taken from their original context and combined with other practices and relationships at different times and in different places. An example of this is the way that some elements of Eastern philosophies and practices such as yoga and meditation have been incorporated into some 'New Age' beliefs.

Gellner sees a place for religion in contemporary society and introduces the concept of 'constitutional religion'. This is developed from the idea of 'constitutional monarchy', in which the symbols and rituals of monarchy are retained but the monarchy wields no actual power. An example would be the singing of the hymn 'Abide with me' at the non-religious football cup final to produce a sense of shared tradition and solidarity.

David Lyon believes that ideas of secularisation are misplaced and says that the evidence shows there is a 're-enchantment of the world', and that religion can flourish in postmodern conditions.

Knowledge check 10

Identify two groups that could be used as examples of 'neo-tribalism'.

Some argue that as religion becomes 'packaged' as a commodity on offer in the marketplace, it becomes 'Disneyfied', i.e. trivialised.

In a postmodern world of endless choice and uncertainty, some see the rise of religious **fundamentalism** (see pp. 18–19) as a rational response to 'choice overload', where individuals have to make choices not only among consumer products but also between ideas and values. Fundamentalism offers a return to certainties.

Key concepts

metanarratives; choice; fundamentalism; constitutional religion; Disneyfication

Evaluation

+ Offers an explanation for the increase in the number and nature of religious groups in contemporary society, including sects, cults and New Age practices.
+ Sees the rise of fundamentalism as a rational response to the lack of certainty in postmodern societies.
+ Shows how religion can still offer moral guidance to many.
− Overemphasises the extent to which the old certainties and ideas have collapsed and the degree to which people are faced with 'real' choices.
− Fundamentalism can be seen as a reactionary response to modernism, rather than a postmodern reaction to choice.
− By emphasising the 'playful' perspective, denies the serious way in which many individuals approach religion.

Exam tip

Showing that there is no single agreed position within a particular perspective is a good way of demonstrating the skills of analysis and evaluation.

Feminist perspectives

There are several feminist perspectives on religion, but they share what Abbott and Wallace refer to as 'the female prism'. This refers to women viewing most modern religions as patriarchal institutions, asserting the power of males over females. This claim is based on examining religious beliefs and texts and the roles allocated to women within religious institutions.

Most feminists start from the view that what we know of ancient religions indicates that they celebrated what was regarded as the mystical power of women, and there were powerful female goddesses and priestesses. Male-dominated religions such as Christianity, Islam and Judaism are believed to have suppressed the older, female-orientated religions and relegated women to lesser, subservient roles. While the Roman Catholic Church has 'the cult of Mary', feminists point out that it is Mary, 'alone of all her sex', who is venerated, rather than all females.

Many religious rituals are forbidden to women, or if there are women present, they have to stand apart, emphasising their separate status. In most religions women are not allowed to hold priestly roles, and even where this has happened, as recently within the Church of England, it has been the source of conflict and controversy, with some adherents leaving the church in protest.

Exam tip

Remember that there have been changes in some religions with regard to the role of women. For example, the Church of England now has ordained women ministers and (currently) one female bishop, while 'liberal' Judaism has some women rabbis.

Knowledge check 11

Give an example, from any religion with which you are familiar, of a position or ritual that is forbidden to women.

Alan Aldridge has pointed out how few religions treat men and women equally. Those that might be able to claim this include the Religious Society of Friends (Quakers), Unitarians and Christian Scientists. Aldridge also points out that when the subservient role of women is challenged, the practices tend to be justified in terms of charismatic or traditional authority. Thus arguments based on the right of women to equal treatment are regarded as of lesser importance than justifications based on sacred texts.

Bruce believes that it is not 'simply' **misogyny** that explains the inferior position of women in most religions. He points out that all religions have at the heart of their teachings a profound interest in sexuality and the family. He argues that after centuries of defending and explaining particular patterns of gender relations, religions find it difficult to change their position. He points out that given that it is usually within the family that religious beliefs and traditions are passed down the generations, it is easy to see why fundamentalists in particular would be opposed to changes in gender roles.

Perhaps because of these traditional patterns, many New Religious Movements (NRMs) (see p. 25) have a particular appeal to women. Many NRMs and New Age movements offer women more powerful and liberating roles than do traditional religions, and promote positive images of womanhood. Some of these movements also encourage men to explore the more 'feminine' side of their nature.

> **Misogyny** A deep-seated dislike or hatred of females, and/or prejudicial or discriminatory practices against them.

> **Exam tip**
>
> Make a list of some religious teachings (ideally from more than one religion) that are concerned with sexuality and the family. Lists such as this are very useful when revising, as they provide examples with which to illustrate your arguments and evidence.

Key concepts

the female prism; misogyny; NRMs

Evaluation

+ Draw attention to the patriarchal nature of most religions.
+ Offer some explanation of the continued subservient roles allocated to women within religions.
+ Suggest why more women than men might be attracted to NRMs.
- Don't really explain why the older, female-oriented religions were suppressed.
- The evidence for the roles of women in many NRMs and New Age groups is based on relatively few examples, and it is not clear that more powerful and liberating roles for women are the reason that women join such groups.

Summary

- Religion is a form of ideology.
- Science refers to both a body of knowledge and a method of developing and testing hypotheses.
- When looking at any hypotheses, research or writings on religion, it is important to note which definition is being used.

- Different theories of religion take different viewpoints on the relationship between religion, religious beliefs and the wider society.

■ Religion, social change and social stability

Religion and social change

There is an important debate within sociology regarding whether religion acts, or under certain circumstances can act, as a force for social change, or whether it is primarily a conservative force, helping to maintain the status quo.

The ideas of Max Weber and the relationship between Calvinist beliefs and modern capitalism (see p. 10) are particularly important in showing how religion can act to bring about social change.

Other suggestions of situations where religion can be argued to have been instrumental in bringing about social change include the following:

- The civil rights movement in the USA in the 1960s, which was closely linked with the black preacher Martin Luther King.
- In Latin America in the 1960s and 1970s where radical and even revolutionary groups emerged within the Roman Catholic Church and some priests and nuns took the side of the poor and oppressed against right-wing leaderships. This is referred to as **liberation theology**.
- Islamic fundamentalists brought down the Westernised rule of the Shah of Persia in 1979 and replaced it with the world's first Islamic state, Iran, governed by ayatollahs (high-ranking Shiite religious leaders). A return to conservative values was enforced.
- In the 1980s, the Roman Catholic Church in Poland opposed the Communist regime and supported the Solidarity trade union movement to achieve social change.

Key concepts

Protestant ethic thesis; liberation theology; Islamic fundamentalism

Evaluation

+ Examples show that under certain circumstances, religions and religious ideas can help to bring about social change.
+ Some religious ideas do challenge the status quo.
- It can be argued that these are minority examples and that, in general, the established churches act in the interests of the most powerful group(s) to maintain the existing social order.

Knowledge check 12

Briefly explain what is meant by 'the status quo'.

Liberation theology
A belief that people have a duty to free themselves from social, economic and political oppression in this world, rather than accepting such injustices as divine will.

Exam tip

It is always helpful to support your arguments with relevant examples. It is worth making a separate section in your folder to note examples and, of course, the particular topic or issue for which they might be used. Keep adding to the list throughout your course, and don't forget to look through this section when doing your exam revision.

Religion and social conflict

Where religion is associated with social change, it is often involved in social conflict. Increasingly, global tensions highlight the capacity of religions to threaten or challenge the prevailing social order, often resulting in conflict.

Beckford has pointed out that the risk of serious conflict is highest in parts of the world where deep religious divisions coincide with strong political and social divisions. Examples include conflict between Muslims in north Sudan and Nigeria, and Christians in the south of Sudan and Nigeria.

The huge tensions between Israel and Palestine are at least in part the result of conflicts between Jews and Muslims. Tensions between Hindus and Muslims in India have resulted in recent episodes of violent conflict. Similarly, the long history of conflict between Protestants and Catholics in Northern Ireland has its roots in ethnic and political divisions as well as in religious differences.

An aspect of religious beliefs particularly associated with conflict is **religious fundamentalism**.

Fundamentalism is a rejection of modernity, with a strong desire to impose what are regarded as the traditional beliefs on the whole of society. It is accepted that 'unbelievers' are found not only outside the faith but also within it. Fundamentalist movements can be regarded as inherently totalitarian, in that they seek to make all aspects of society conform to religious laws.

Davie (1989) drew on the work of Marty (1988) to come up with the following ideal type of fundamentalism:

- Fundamentalist groups usually emerge from those holding traditional beliefs that have remained generally unchallenged for many generations.
- Any challenges, which may come from external or internal sources, generate insecurity, which may be addressed by a specific leader.
- The authority to challenge the 'new' ideas or customs usually comes from a sacred text or book.
- An 'us and them' mentality sets in which may pitch the group against the rest of society.
- Even though fundamentalist groups are against modernity, they often use modern technologies to spread their message.

Fundamentalists can be found in many different religions. Fundamentalist movements exist in Christianity, Islam, Judaism, Hinduism and Sikhism. Many, however, see fundamentalism not only as an aspect of traditional religiosity but as an inherently political movement, often involving, and of particular appeal to, those members of a society who are, or who consider themselves to be, socially, economically or politically oppressed.

Fundamentalism may be expressed in different ways. Some fundamentalists try to bring about social change through political means, such as the right-wing Christian evangelicals (sometimes referred to as the New Christian Right) allied to the American Republican Party, who oppose what they see as wrongful social policies such as gay rights, same-sex marriage and abortion.

> **Religious fundamentalism** A belief that there is a need to return to what are regarded as the original beliefs and practices of the religion, usually thought to reside in the sacred texts, such as the Bible, the Torah, the Talmud and the Quran.

> **Knowledge check 13**
>
> Give an example of a modern technology used by a fundamentalist group.

However, other fundamentalist groups are associated with often violent conflicts. Examples include militant religious Zionists in Israel, Hamas in Palestine, the Lord's Resistance Army in Uganda, Boko Haram in Nigeria and Al Qaeda and Daesh (so-called Islamic State) in the Middle East.

In Judaism, members of the ultra-Orthodox Zionist movement seek to separate themselves not only from Gentiles (non-Jews) but from other Jews who do not follow the religious laws as strictly as they do. Following the Six-Day War between the Israelis and the Arab states of Egypt, Jordan and Syria in 1967, many Zionists moved to the occupied (or as they see it 'liberated') territories on the West Bank, the Gaza Strip and the Golan Heights, leading to frequent conflict especially with Palestinians.

Of particular concern to Western governments, however, is the so-called Islamic fundamentalism. Under this broad (and contested) umbrella term, there have been terrorist attacks on civilians in many different countries. Members of groups such as Al Qaeda, Hamas, Boko Haram and Daesh consider that they are engaged in a Jihad (holy war) against Western domination of the Muslim world.

> **Exam tip**
>
> Showing that you recognise that there are different types of fundamentalist groups will demonstrate knowledge, analysis and evaluation.

Key concepts

sacred texts; modernity; traditional values; evangelicals

Evaluation

+ Can be seen as a reaction against postmodernity in which all metanarratives have been undermined.
+ Can be seen as a challenge to established religious beliefs and practices invoking a re-examination of the founding texts.
+ Represents an authentic religious response to increasing secularisation.
− The term 'fundamentalism' was originally used to refer to a movement in American Protestantism — it is not necessarily appropriate to apply it to other, especially non-Western, religions.
− Some people question the extent to which fundamentalism has actually grown. The very visible nature of some events may make such movements seem more numerous and powerful than they actually are.

Religion and social stability

The idea that religion brings, or can bring, social stability is related to functionalist ideas that religion serves to integrate the members of society into a shared value system. However, it goes further by claiming that religion seeks to defend the political and social status quo. This means that this view of religion sees it as an essentially conservative force in society.

The Hindu caste system, based on religious beliefs, was a system of social stratification that served for more than 1,000 years to maintain strict social divisions in society and acted against change. Although now outlawed, its consequences remain, and are particularly detrimental to those at the bottom of the system — the 'outcasts' or 'untouchables', now known as Dalits.

The relationship between religion and social stability is at least partly based on the links in many societies between the state and a specific religion. In such cases, the established religion is often granted certain privileges, and there are usually connections between leading political and religious leaders. The established, or state, church in England is the Church of England, with the reigning monarch as the Supreme Governor.

The classic example of the fusion of religious and political power is in the Vatican State in Italy, where the Pope wields both **temporal** and spiritual power. The Pope is both head of the Roman Catholic Church worldwide and a head of state — 'sovereign of the Vatican City state'.

Some claim that an example of religion acting as a conservative force was that of Methodism in the eighteenth and nineteenth centuries in Britain. In what has come to be known as 'the age of revolutions', it is suggested that the Methodist movement, which was very popular among the English working classes, helped to prevent revolutionary movements growing in England. There is some evidence to support this, as John Wesley, a co-founder of the Methodist movement in the eighteenth century, attempted to instil into his followers deference towards established social and religious authorities. Thomas Allen, a Methodist solicitor granted an audience with the prime minister in 1812, is reported as having told him that 'members of our Society consider themselves as members of the Establishment and do not choose to rank with Dissenters'.

It is notable that some people are able to claim allegiance to the conservative values of their religion while acting in ways that are contrary to those values. Examples are the considerable number of Roman Catholics who use contraception, Catholic women from the Republic of Ireland (where abortion is illegal except under certain circumstances) coming to England to have terminations, and Catholics who have divorced and remarried. There is a movement in the Roman Catholic Church to allow remarried divorcees to receive Holy Communion, which is currently denied them.

Research carried out by the Pew Research Center in 2015 among Roman Catholics in the USA showed that, despite the teachings of the church, the following percentages thought that the behaviours listed below were **not** sinful:

- homosexuality — 39% (rising to 51% among those below the age of 30)
- living together outside of marriage — 54%
- getting a divorce — 61%
- using artificial contraception — 66%

Clemence (2015) conducted an analysis of various longitudinal British surveys to discover the strength of heterodox religious beliefs, such as belief in foretelling the future, horoscopes, ghosts, telepathy, etc. He found that a near-majority of those surveyed believed in foretelling the future, around a quarter believed in horoscopes, about a third believed in ghosts, and 10–15 per cent believed in black magic and the possibility of exchanging messages with the dead. Perhaps his most surprising finding was that those who held **orthodox religious beliefs** were more likely to hold heterodox beliefs than those without orthodox beliefs.

Knowledge check 14

Give an example of how some members of the Church of England have formal political power.

Temporal power of the papacy Refers to the political and secular activity of popes as distinguished from their religious and pastoral role.

Orthodox religious beliefs Those that follow or conform to the accepted rules and beliefs of a religion or philosophy. Heterodox beliefs are those that are not in accordance with the established or accepted rules or beliefs.

It is sometimes suggested, however, that it is the very conservatism of many religions that draws people to them, as the freedom and individuality of postmodern society leave them searching for stability.

It is worth noting that it is not always easy to fit a particular religious movement into a particular category. Examples such as the Iranian revolution, ISIS and the Taliban can be seen as radical and revolutionary in their attempts to bring about religious and political change, but also as conservative in their desire to make their societies return to what are seen as traditional values.

Key concepts

dominant value system; status quo; established religion; conservatism

Evaluation

+ The emphasis on tradition and continuity has a wide appeal in conditions of rapid change.
+ State religions link religious beliefs and practices to allegiance to the state, helping to explain the absence of revolutionary movements.
- Conservative religious bodies allied to certain nation states have resulted in their defending and supporting ruthless regimes and practices that ignore human rights.
- Unquestioning support for the status quo hampers progress in many areas of life, for example equal rights for women and gay people.
- Clinging to traditional values in a changing world can cause much unhappiness, as people struggle to reconcile their religious faith with their preferred way of life.

Summary

- Religions and religious beliefs can act as a force for social change.
- They can also act to maintain social stability and preserve the status quo.
- Some religious groups are radical in that they attempt to overthrow a particular regime or set of values, but conservative in that once established, they attempt, sometimes by force, to bring that society back to 'traditional values'.
- Religions can also act as a source of social conflict, either between different religions or within the same religion.

Religious organisations

In order better to study religious organisations and how they might differ in their structure, roles, beliefs and practices, sociologists have attempted to classify them into broad groups. This is helpful, but it is important to remember that often such classifications are 'rough guides' — what Weber would call 'ideal types' — and it is not always easy or even possible to place a particular group into one of the categories. Equally important is the fact that many classifications, particularly the earlier ones, were developed in respect of the Christian religion, and it is not easy, or often even helpful, to try to apply the distinctions to other religious faiths.

It is suggested that all religions and religious groups offer spiritual 'compensators' to their members, i.e. some kind of reward for believing and belonging. Compensators obviously differ between groups, but include heaven, personal fulfilment, comfort in times of grief and distress, control over evil influences, and the achievement of worldly success.

Max Weber and Ernst Troeltsch were the first sociologists to attempt a classification of religious organisations, and their distinction was between churches and sects. Sociologists since then have developed other classifications.

Churches

When we speak of 'a church' we do not, of course, refer only to the building in which religious worship occurs. Also included in the concept are the organisation, beliefs, rituals and membership. The 'community of believers' is often worldwide, as is the structure and organisation.

Churches are deemed to have the following characteristics:

- A formal organisational structure with a hierarchy of paid officials.
- Membership that is open to everyone.
- Membership is usually 'ascribed' — that is, members are born into the church, though some will be converts. Being baptised into the church brings about 'salvation through grace'.
- Churches sometimes enable religious diversity by creating groups within the church, e.g. orders of monks and nuns, thus trying to avoid groups breaking away (schism).
- Positive attitudes towards, and often close links with, the state and the established order, sometimes resulting in ideologies to defend and legitimise the status quo, e.g. 'the divine right of kings'.

Exam tip

That the classification of religious groups was based on the Christian religion and that it is not always helpful to apply it to other religions is an important point that could gain marks for analysis and evaluation.

Knowledge check 15

Briefly explain what Weber meant by an 'ideal type'.

....

The 'divine right of kings' A doctrine that stated that the authority of the monarch came directly from God, and that monarchs were not subject to any earthly authority, such as from Parliament.

Sects

The term covers a wide variety of religious organisations. Their nature has changed over time, but again, an attempt has been made to find common characteristics.

Many early sects emerged as direct challenges to the established church, as schismatic or splinter groups that disagreed with certain doctrines. They were often protesting against what they saw as 'modernising' influences. Stark and Bainbridge (1973) said that 'sects claim to be authentic, purged versions of the faith from which they split'.

Characteristics of sects include the following:
- At least initially, they tend to be small, and are often led by a charismatic leader.
- They hold a belief that only their members will be 'saved' through their personal commitment and adherence to a particular lifestyle — 'salvation through faith'.
- Membership is often through a personal spiritual experience.
- Members often have to adhere to a strict moral code.
- Members are often drawn from the lower social classes.
- There is sometimes an oppositional relationship to the state.

Given the diversity of sects, their beliefs and their organisational structure, Wilson (1961) developed a typology of sects to help to distinguish different types:
- Conversionist — sects that try to change the world, e.g. The Salvation Army.
- Adventist — sects that are awaiting some kind of divine intervention, usually the 'Second Coming' of the Messiah, e.g. Jehovah's Witnesses.
- Introversionist — sects that withdraw, and often live apart from the wider society in order to develop members' 'inner spirituality', such as the Amish.

Wilson also identified four sects that did not emerge as a result of a schism from an established church, had strong but not charismatic leaders, did not become a denomination, and shared the following characteristics:
- They exist in tension with the wider society.
- They impose tests of merit on would-be members.
- They exercise stern discipline on the lives of members, imposing sanctions on those who deviate — sometimes leading to expulsion.
- They demand a sustained and total commitment to the group.

These sects were the Seventh Day Adventists, the Jehovah's Witnesses, the Exclusive Brethren, and the Christadelphians.

Denominations

Denominations are often said to fall somewhere between a church and a sect. Some denominations, e.g. Methodists, developed from sects. However, this is not an inevitable process.

Denominations have overcome one of the problems faced by some sects, particularly those led by a charismatic leader, namely how to ensure the survival of the group after the death of the leader. Denominations have developed a more formal set of rules to ensure succession and also a hierarchical structure — in Weber's words, they have become 'routinised'.

Knowledge check 16

Briefly explain what is meant by a 'charismatic leader'.

Denominations are usually tolerant of the wider society and accept a lower level of commitment from members than do most sects.

An important issue that leads some sects towards more routinised forms of worship is that of infant baptism. While sects emphasise adult admission to the group, often through adult baptism, members of denominations want their children to be brought up in the faith. This has led them to adopt the practice of infant baptism, a feature which makes denominations more like a church.

Unlike sects and churches, denominations take a non-universalist approach to salvation — that is, they accept that there are other ways to salvation than through membership of their organisation.

Cults

Although the terms 'sect' and 'cult' are often used interchangeably, it is helpful to identify some differences between them.

Cults tend to be the least formally structured form of religious group. Many of them started as a private form of religion, often with a mystical dimension. It is not always necessary to 'join' the cult in any formal sense — one may simply accept the ideas and teachings of the leader. Cults do not usually have any previous ties with a religious group — they tend to be innovative.

Stark and Bainbridge (1985) identified three different types of cult:

- Audience cults — these are the least formally organised. There are often no regular gatherings, and the 'audience' subscribes to the doctrine through the mediums of literature, film, etc. Examples would be believers in astrology or UFOs.
- Client cults — these tend to be more organised than audience cults. They often offer therapeutic compensators, e.g. claiming to cure mental disease, bring about calm and serenity, help in achieving worldly success. Stark and Bainbridge say that the relationship between the deliverers of the doctrine and the recipients 'closely resembles the relationship between therapist and patient or between consultant and client'. Commitment remains partial and clients may even belong to other religious groups at the same time. Examples of client cults would be Dianetics and Transcendental Meditation.
- Cult movements — these are fully fledged religious organisations that attempt to satisfy all the spiritual needs of their members. They demand high levels of commitment, even complete submission to the demands of the cult. Examples would be Heaven's Gate, Order of the Solar Temple, the Manson Family.

Classification of churches, sects, denominations and cults

Wallis classifies the above according to whether the wider society sees them as being respectable (churches and denominations) or deviant (sects and cults) and also as to whether they see themselves as being the only road to salvation (churches and sects) or not (denominations and cults).

Knowledge check 17

Give an example of a denomination, other than Methodists.

Exam tip

You will always be rewarded for relevant examples. It is worth making a list in your folder of all the different types of religious grouping and noting a few examples of each — you will find several in your textbooks. You may find that some groups can appear in more than one classification, but learn the examples so that you can use them appropriately in an exam.

Knowledge check 18

Give two examples of how the Church of England might be thought to be 'respectable'.

Key concepts

compensators; ideal types; salvation; routinisation; non-universalism

Evaluation

+ Identifies key characteristics of religious organisations, showing similarities and differences between them.
+ Focuses on the social dimension of religions, including their relationship to the rest of society.
+ Makes some attempt to locate religious organisations in their historical context.
+ Shows how some religious organisations may develop over time.
- Some classifications are more appropriate to an earlier period of history, where emerging Protestant groups were in opposition to a dominant Roman Catholic Church.
- Not always easy or possible to take account of the dynamics of groups and how they have changed over time.
- Often very difficult to locate a religious group in a particular category, especially secretive and more ephemeral groups such as some cults.
- Sects are less persecuted than in the past and may now have a less oppositional relationship to the state.
- Not all sects are led by a charismatic leader, and not all sects have a particularly strong appeal to members of the working class.

New Religious Movements

New Religious Movements (NRMs) is a term adopted to describe the proliferation of new religious groups throughout the world and is thought to be more neutral than terms such as 'sect' or 'cult'. Barker (2011) defines an NRM as 'a movement that has a membership consisting primarily of converts'.

The very fact that the term covers such a wide variety of groups makes classifications of NRMs difficult, but attempts have been made.

Wallis (1984) developed one of the most frequently used typologies of NRMs. It was based on the group's relationship to the wider society. He concluded that NRMs could be placed into one of three main categories:

- World-affirming — such groups accept the goals and values of the wider society, and offer members ways of achieving personal success. They are unlike many religious movements in that there is usually no theology or ritual, and members live 'normal' lives within society, attending meetings or gatherings when required or desired. An example is Transcendental Meditation (TM).
- World-accommodating — these groups are often an offshoot of an established church. Typically, they neither reject nor embrace the world, but work towards restoring the spiritual purity they consider the main body of the church to have lost. They sometimes believe that members have special gifts, such as prophecy or

Exam tip

It is important to show that you recognise the considerable variety of religious movements that have been placed under the banner of NRMs. This will not, of course, prevent you from discussing the various classifications that have been suggested, and you should try to mention examples in each category.

glossolalia (the ability to 'speak in tongues'). Examples are the New Pentecostalists and the New Charismatics.

- World-rejecting — these groups completely reject the world around them, believing it to be evil and corrupt. They expect followers to withdraw from wider society, to a greater or lesser degree, and some of them have authoritarian regimes. Examples are the People's Temple, the Unification Church ('Moonies'), Branch Davidian.

Beckford (1986) considers that there is a strong relationship between the emergence of NRMs and rapid social change. He suggests that NRMs share the following characteristics:

- They tend to attract public attention for disseminating ideas and practices that are more specialised and **esoteric** than those of established religions.
- They tend to allow lay people (those without a formal religious role) to participate more fully in their activities.
- They often offer participants encouragement to translate spirituality into practical, everyday activities.

As examples, Beckford offers Rastafarians, with their largely political agenda in Jamaica, the missionary element of the ISKCON (Hare Krishna) movement in India, and the psycho-social benefits promised by Scientology in the USA and elsewhere.

Barker (2011) suggests that most NRMs share the following characteristics:

- As their members are converts, they tend to be more enthusiastic and active than those born into a religion.
- They are likely to appeal to an atypical sample of the population — usually younger and often from a middle-class background.
- They are usually led by a founder accorded a charismatic status by the followers. This means that the leader is unrestricted by rules or traditions.
- Many NRMs, especially those falling into the 'world-rejecting' category, have relatively **dichotomous** world views that draw a sharp distinction between godly and satanic, good and bad, and 'them and us'.
- Following from this, tensions are likely to arise between the group and the wider society.
- NRMs change far more rapidly and radically than older, more established religions. Inevitably, the charismatic founders will die and the initial converts will age, therefore the demographic composition of the movements will undergo a marked transformation.

Another aspect of NRMs is that many of them have been, or will be, relatively short-lived. Rodney Stark (1996) wrote: 'Probably no more than one religious movement out of a hundred will attract more than 100,000 followers and last for as long as a century.'

Who joins NRMs?

Stark and Bainbridge (1985) found that there were two characteristics of those who joined NRMs:

- a social grievance
- a strong interpersonal bond with the person or persons who recruited them.

Exam tip

Try to give at least one example when you are discussing different classifications of NRMs.

Esoteric Refers to things or ideas that are understood or intended for only a small, select number of people who have a specialised knowledge or interest.

Dichotomy A model that splits something into two opposites.

Exam tip

Your class notes and textbooks will doubtless give several examples of other ways of classifying NRMs. It is important to be able to name some, but it is unlikely that you will need to go into great detail. What is important is that you are able to show analysis and evaluation by pointing out the various problems of classifying so many diverse groups, but also the ways in which such classifications may be helpful.

Cadell Last (2012) of the American Humanist Association said that later research had found additional characteristics of NRMs and their members. These were:

- pre-existing social networks (friends recruited friends, family members recruited other family members)
- the development of strong social bonds between members
- existing members engaged in intensive daily interaction with new members to keep up their commitment
- weak external social ties — few friends outside the group
- no or weak experience of or affiliation to another religion
- members were 'seekers' — seeking answers to the 'big questions' in life
- members wanted direct rewards, such as self-esteem and/or a sense of power and control.

Some NRMs that start by being in tension with the wider society gradually adapt: the 'them and us' characteristic declines and they become more like other, conventional, religious movements. This process is called 'denominationalisation'. It can be applied to the Society of Friends (Quakers), though it is important to stress that this process happens in relatively few movements and is by no means inevitable.

New Age Movements

Unlike most formal religions, New Age Movements (NAMs) have no holy text, no central organisation, no formal membership, no ordained ministers and no central body of belief. This means that the term 'New Age Movements' serves as a kind of umbrella grouping together quite diverse groups.

New Age Movements developed in the Western world in the 1970s. They are seen as a form of alternative NRM, with a focus on such diverse concerns as inner spirituality, the environment, spiritualism, mysticism, astrology, paganism and magic. Their beliefs and practices are so diverse that some have argued that it is difficult to think of them in terms of a 'movement' at all. While many people hold some what might be termed 'new age' beliefs, such as the importance of protecting the environment or a belief in alternative forms of healing, actual membership of New Age groups is small.

Bruce (1991) sees such groups as characterised by 'eclecticism', meaning that they bring together a variety of beliefs. However, they almost all have a focus on the 'inner self' and the belief that there is a need to turn inwards to retrieve and develop 'inner wisdom'. Many NAMs are characterised by their commercialism and there is a healthy market in books, magazines, crystals and other items with 'healing properties' or the ability to work magic.

The relationship between different social groups and religious movements is further discussed on pp. 29–35.

Key concepts

New Religious Movements; world-affirming; world-accommodating; world-rejecting; New Age Movements; eclecticism; denominationalisation

---

Knowledge check 19

Why might someone with weak external ties be attracted to an NRM?

Exam tip

It is important when discussing NRMs to show awareness of the different types. For example, the lists above are more relevant to world-rejecting movements than to world-accommodating ones.

Exam tip

If a question asks about NAMs, show that you know that the term covers a wide variety of groups.

Evaluation

+ NRMs, as a wider term than sects or cults, are a more appropriate way of defining the many new religious groups that have developed since the latter part of the twentieth century.
+ NRMs have met a religious or spiritual need for some who might not have engaged with mainstream religions.
+ Some NRMs have caused mainstream religions to reflect on their basic values and the extent to which these are still reflected in their beliefs and practices.
− The terms NRMs and NAMs cover such a wide variation of movements that it is often difficult to fit some groups into a particular classification.
− Some NRMs have caused public concerns over their controlling tendencies, particularly those in which members have harmed themselves or others.
− Not all NRMs have a particular appeal to the working class, nor do all members join out of a sense of deprivation.

Summary

- There are various ways of classifying religious organisations.
- While classifications are helpful, they are ideal types, and many organisations and groups do not fit easily into classifications.
- Most religious organisations experience greater or lesser changes over time, so may fit more easily into a classification at one stage of their development than another.
- Some groups are secretive and/or hostile to outsiders, so knowledge of these may be partial.
- Most classifications apply only to Christian groups and it is difficult and often unwise to apply them to other religions.
- There has been a growth in both NRMs and NAMs since the mid-twentieth century.

■Religious/spiritual organisations and social groups

The 2011 Census asked people about their religion. The question was voluntary, but only 7% did not answer. For England and Wales, these were the replies given:

- Christian   59%
- Muslim   5%
- Other   4%
- Not stated   7%
- No religion   25%.

These figures show that almost six out of ten people in England and Wales describe their religion as Christian. However, comparison with the 2001 Census shows the following:

- The proportion stating that they had 'no religion' rose from 14.8% to 25.1%.
- The proportion stating that they were Christian fell from 71.7% to 59.3%.
- All 'other' religions increased — the largest increase being among Muslims, from 3.0% to 4.8%.

Knowledge check 20

Given the fall in church attendance, why might the figure for those saying that they are Christian be so high?

Religion and social class

Historically in Britain there was a fairly close relationship between social class and religious participation. In the postmodern world this relationship has fragmented, and a number of researchers and social surveys have found that social class is less important than other factors such as age, ethnicity and gender as indicators of both religious belief and practice.

For Marx, religion was man-made and ideological, and was an instrument of the bourgeoisie used to confirm the right of the rich to their wealth and privilege and to persuade the working class to accept their inferior position in society.

Weber introduced the concept of the **ideology of disprivilege** to explain the attraction of certain sects to the working class, as they taught that earthly sufferings were a test of faith, and that the poor would receive salvation and rewards in the afterlife. Weber also wrote of the theodicy of good fortune, or privilege, found in religious organisations which offered explanations for the earthly wealth and success enjoyed by some people. World-affirming groups such as Scientology and the Alpha Course, with their promise of how to achieve worldly success, have a particular appeal to the middle classes. Similarly, many Christian evangelical sects draw their membership primarily from the poorer sections of society. Steve Bruce also points out that New Age Movements have a primarily middle-class (and female) membership, as only the relatively well-off can afford the time and money to devote to their practices.

Ideology of disprivilege
Refers to religious explanations which legitimise earthly inequalities. The term is also found as the theodicy of disprivilege.

The **British Social Attitudes** (BSA) survey of 2012 found relatively little difference in the socioeconomic class of those who never attend religious services. Using the NS-SEC classification, the survey found that 63.3% of the salariat said that they never attended a religious service, while the figure rose to 67.9% of the working class.

However, an online YouGov poll conducted in September 2014, covering 7,212 adults aged 16-plus, found that of those who *were* regular attenders at religious services, 63% were middle-class (ABC1) and 38% were working-class (C2DE).

Field (2014) found that more people from the AB social group were regular readers of the Bible than those from the DE group. However, Clemence (2014) found that those of higher economic status were less likely to hold traditional religious beliefs (e.g. belief in God, life after death) than those of lower economic status, giving some slight support for the 'deprivation' thesis.

Religion and gender

Much research has shown that on almost all indicators of religiosity, women are more 'religious' than men. That is, they are more likely than men to believe in God and life after death, attend religious services, pray and read the Bible regularly. On average, 65% of the members of congregations at UK churches are women.

A report published in 2015 with findings from the 1970 *British Cohort Study* based on 9,000 people showed that 34% of women were self-reported atheists or agnostics compared with 54% of men, and 36% of women said that they did not believe in life after death compared with 63% of men. Data from the *British Social Attitudes* survey of 2013 found that 57.3% of men reported that they had no religion, compared with 44.4% of women.

Several explanations have been put forward for such differences in religiosity.
- Traditionally, mothers have the major role in child-rearing, and see church-going and church activities as part of their role of instilling moral values in their children.
- When many women did not work outside the home, they had more time for church-going during the week.
- There are different patterns of socialisation for males and females, with males socialised to be more aggressive and rational, while females are encouraged to develop their emotional side, making them more receptive to issues of morality.
- Until recently, men and women operated in very different spheres — the socially gendered division of labour led to their having different structural locations, with men more exposed to the wider society through their work and women more confined to the domestic sphere. Men were thus more likely to pick up new ideas and attitudes, such as those concerned with growing secularisation.

Trzebiatowska and Bruce (2012) looked at gender differences in religiosity (primarily in Western Christianity) and developed the idea of different and separate social spheres for males and females. They suggest that the traditionally different social roles of men and women meant that men were influenced by the growing secularisation of society before women were. This led to men leaving or drifting

Exam tip

When quoting findings from social surveys, show that you are aware that the different methods of survey data collection each have their weaknesses.

Knowledge check 21

State two potential disadvantages of online surveys.

Exam tip

As with all explanations of social phenomena, you should be able to discuss any problems or weaknesses in the arguments. If you look at the list on the left, you should be able to find some criticisms that could be made of them.

away from religion, meaning that congregations increasingly became dominated by women. The consequence of this is that Christianity is becoming a 'gendered religion'. The preponderance of women in congregations and church activities had a 'snowball effect', with men becoming ever less likely to become involved in what was increasingly seen as a female sphere. Trzebiatowska and Bruce consider that there is a 'time lag' occurring, and conclude that as women's roles in society become increasingly similar to those of men, the gender gap in religion will shrink.

The 'feminisation' of the church has occurred in other ways. Women increasingly play important leadership roles. The first women priests in the Church of England were ordained in 1994, and there are now more female than male **ordinands**.

However, most of the literature about the gendered nature of religion relates to Western Christianity. A closer look at other religions shows that among Jews, Muslims and Hindus, men are more religious than women, at least in terms of their attendance at services of worship. This casts doubt on the assumption that women are inherently more religious than men, and draws attention to social and cultural factors.

While Islam teaches that men and women are morally equal in the sight of God, women have not had, and frequently do not have, equal access to many areas of Islamic life. However, many of the restrictions placed on Muslim women are cultural in origin, rather than based on religious teachings. Many Muslim women are now challenging traditional attitudes and actively seeking to play a different role in both their faith and the wider society.

Religion and age

Age is one of the most important social factors associated with religiosity. The 2011 Census showed that one in five Christians is now aged 65 or over. With regard to Christianity in the UK, and the main Christian churches in particular, attendance at religious services shows a strong bias towards the upper age groups. Recent surveys have found that the average age of congregations is 62, while in rural areas it is 65. With the number of young people attending church falling, and only one in ten children now being baptised into the Christian faith, it is unlikely that this trend will be reversed.

The Roman Catholic Church has shown less of a decline, but its congregations, particularly in urban areas, have been bolstered by the arrival of immigrants from the primarily Catholic countries of Eastern Europe, particularly Poland.

A different age profile is shown by evangelical churches, particularly those whose membership is drawn primarily from black and immigrant groups. A panel of more than 1800 members of evangelical churches in 2013 revealed that 61% said their church had 'lots of children' at services, and only 26% said their congregation was 'predominantly elderly'.

The 2011 Census replies showed that the highest proportions of self-reported Christians were in the 45–69 age group, while the highest proportions of self-reported Muslims were in the 20–39 age groups, reflecting the younger overall demographic of

Ordinand A person training to be a priest or a minister of religion.

Exam tip

It is important to be able to make at least brief comparisons between different faiths when discussing gender and religiosity. In particular, the role of women in Islam varies considerably between societies.

Knowledge check 22

Why might evangelical churches, whose membership is drawn primarily from black and immigrant groups, have a different age profile from Anglican congregations?

the Muslim population. Of those reporting that they had 'no religion', four in ten were aged under 25, and four in five were under 50.

With regard to the mainstream Christian churches, it seems likely that the fall in both members and congregations will continue as older members and worshippers die and do not seem likely to be replaced by younger people. Evangelical churches might fare better, as they seem more able to retain younger members. It is also likely that Muslim congregations will not decline as rapidly as some other groups, as in many cases their religion is an essential part of their ethnic identity.

Reasons given for the age profile of the main Christian churches include that their older members grew up in a more 'religious' age than at present, where Sunday school and church attendance were far more prevalent than today. Those born and growing up in a more secular age seem less likely to identify with, and practise, a religious faith, with the probable exception of those in evangelical churches and from black and minority ethnic (BME) backgrounds.

Data from the 2013 *British Social Attitudes* survey can be used to look at the age profile of women who said that they had no religion — the so-called religious 'nones'. While only 14.6% of women aged 75 and older were in this category, the proportions were much higher for younger women — for example 52.9% of those aged 35–44 and 60.8% of those in the 18–24 age group.

Eileen Barker (2011) looked at how several NRMs that emerged around the 1970s were coping with an ageing membership. She points out that there are two main ways for an organisation to preserve a younger age profile. One is the birth of a second or even third generation, as the original members have families, and the other is by the recruitment of younger members.

With regard to the first, several NRMs (e.g. the Children of God and the Unification Church) found that children born into the movement left as soon as possible, so this is a far from reliable way of keeping a movement going.

With regard to the second, converts, which is what most members of NRMs are, have a tendency to attract and recruit people of their own age. This explains the young age profile of new movements, but also means that as the original members age, so do new converts. Barker concludes that this process will result in some movements possibly dying out by the end of the century. Many movements, particularly millenarian ones, have made no provision for looking after ageing members, and the members themselves, as a result of their lifestyle within the movement, have made no provision for themselves.

Barker comes to the conclusion that the longer a religious movement has been in existence, the more likely it is to have faced the problems of an ageing membership and to have developed strategies to deal with the issue.

Religion and ethnicity

The term 'ethnic' is usually used to define or describe a group of people sharing a common cultural heritage. Religion is an important component of any cultural heritage, but it is more important to some groups than to others, or more important at one period than another.

Exam tip

While you will not be expected to remember exact percentages in an exam, it is helpful to show a rough idea of proportions — for example, you could say that the BSA survey data showed that while just over 1 in 10 women were religious 'nones', the figure was over 6 out of 10 for 18–24-year-olds. If you can't remember any figures at all, at least make sure that you could say that the proportion of women claiming no religion fell with every increase in age group.

Millenarian movement
One that believes that there will be a significant event, usually the Second Coming of Christ, that will change the world order and lead to 1000 years of blessedness. The event that will trigger this is often thought to be imminent, and the members believe they will be among the 'saved'.

Knowledge check 23

Suggest two ways in which a religious organisation might make provision for ageing members.

Issues of religion and ethnicity are often discussed in the context of immigrants, whether first-generation or not, who may have a different religion, as well as a different cultural heritage, from at least the majority of members of the host society. Sociologists have been interested to find out how important religion is as part of the overall identity, particularly of those from minority ethnic groups. One interesting finding is that members of these groups often seem able to hold and manage multiple identities, e.g. as a Pakistani, a Muslim and a British citizen.

One important question has been what happens to both religious and ethnic identities with regard to second- and third-generation immigrants.

Nandi and Platt (2014) used data from the *Wave 2 Understanding Society* research to analyse a sample of people aged 60 and under with regard to the strength of their religious and ethnic identity. All the people in the findings below were British-born, i.e. those from minority ethnic populations were at least second-generation immigrants. The 'White Christian' group is included for purposes of comparison, and the percentages have been weighted to represent the distribution of the groups in the population as a whole.

Strength of religious and ethnic identity by selected ethno-religious groups		
Group	Religion is important (%)	Ethnicity is important (%)
Pakistani Muslim	85	51
Bangladeshi Muslim	79	47
Indian Muslim	78	42
Indian Sikh	66	48
African Christian	57	56
Indian Hindu	50	42
Other Christian	38	38
Caribbean Christian	37	59
White Christian	26	15

Source: Adapted from Nandi, A. and Platt, L. (2014) 'A note on ethnicity and identity', *Understanding Society*, January.

The authors conclude that religious identity is very important for most minority ethno-religious groups, and is markedly stronger than ethnic identity, with the exception of Caribbean Christians. There is a greater tendency for Muslims to assert the importance of their religion to their identity. The data also show that religious and ethnic identities are more important to British-born minorities than to the majority population, though there is substantial variation across ethnic groups.

Religious institutions can also be very important for first-generation immigrants, as not only do they offer the comfort of shared, familiar rituals but they often provide a variety of social and welfare services to help their members cope with the various difficulties of settling in a strange country.

Some writers have spoken of the possibility of a 'religious revival' and an increase in religious identification among second and subsequent generations, particularly in the Muslim community, but there does not seem to be any evidence to support this. In fact, Platt (2013) found that across all religious groups the generational pattern seemed to be one of 'assimilation', or a gradual secularity, and there is so far

Exam tip

Being able to state that the importance of religious identity is, for many British-born members of minority ethnic groups, more important than ethnic identity, and also to show that there are differences between different groups, would gain you important marks for both analysis and evaluation.

Knowledge check 24

What does it mean to say that a sample is 'weighted'?

no evidence that Muslims will experience a different pattern. However, given that religious affiliation and religiosity among Muslims start at high initial levels, any secularising process is likely to be slower than for some other groups. Scourfield *et al.* (2012), however, suggest that some generational shifts might be 'reversible', i.e. the children of non-practising parents might assert a religious faith. An example of this might be those young Muslim women whose mothers no longer wear the veil deciding that they will wear it.

Another group who might be thought to have a strong ethno-religious identity are the Jews. It is estimated that there are just under 1 million Jews in the UK, making it the second largest Jewish community in Europe. The two ways of acquiring Jewish identity are by having a Jewish mother or by conversion.

A study published in 2014 looked at elements of 'Jewishness' (David Graham *et al.*, 'Jews in the UK'). Their sample was 3,736 Jews and members of their households. Respondents were asked how important or otherwise they considered 20 different items were to their sense of identity. The top characteristic, considered 'very' or 'fairly' important by 92% of respondents, was 'strong moral and ethical behaviour'. Meanwhile, four out of the five bottom items, cited as 'very' or 'fairly' important by fewer than half of respondents, were religiously oriented. These were 'believing in God', '**keeping kosher**' and 'studying Jewish religious texts'.

These findings suggest that moral and cultural factors are more important than religious ones to a sense of Jewish identity. However, the survey also showed that younger Jews (those under 40) were more religiously observant than middle-aged and elderly Jews. This is attributed to the rise in the number of the ultra-observant Orthodox Jews and the fact that they have much higher birth rates than other Jews.

Overall, the world's population of Jews is declining, and this includes Europe. The Holocaust reduced the Jewish population of Europe from 9.5 million to 3.8 million between 1939 and 1945, but since then there have been rising levels of emigration from Europe, partly due to the increase in levels of anti-Semitism. The overall reason for the decline in the world's Jewish population is a demographic one — more Jews are dying than Jewish babies are being born. Another factor is that Jewishness is passed down only through the maternal line — if a Jewish man marries a non-Jew, their children will not be classed as Jews.

Key concepts

social class; ethnicity; ideology of disprivilege; social spheres; gendered religion; millenarianism; ethno-religious groups

Exam tip

Being able to show that Jewry does not appear to follow the trend found in many religions of younger members being more secular than older ones is an important point — though you should also be able to give the reasons for this.

Keeping kosher Means to obey the Jewish dietary laws.

Exam tip

The Jewish faith is seldom mentioned by students in discussions of minority faiths. Provided that it is relevant to the question, it is a useful thing to include.

Evaluation

+ It is useful to examine the composition of religious groups with reference to class, gender, age and ethnicity.
+ The Marxist concept of ideology and the Weberian concept of the ideology of disprivilege are helpful in analysing the links between religion and social class.
+ There are helpful explanations for the feminisation of the Christian church.
+ Age is one of the most important social factors associated with different levels of religiosity.
+ Research can provide useful predictions of how different types of religious organisation will deal with ageing populations.
+ Research shows the importance of religious identity to many minority ethnic groups.
+ It is important to look at how religious beliefs and practice might differ between first-generation immigrants and subsequent generations.
− The relationship between religion and social class is less pronounced than it used to be.
− Some of the explanations of the apparently greater religiosity of women are outdated in terms of women's roles.
− There is no evidence of a 'religious revival' among UK-born Muslim immigrants.

Summary

- Membership of religious groups and organisations varies by social class, gender, age and ethnicity.
- Particularly in the Christian church, age appears to be the most important factor in explaining different levels of religiosity.
- Many NRMs, especially millenarian movements, are facing difficulties in dealing with an ageing membership.
- Religious identity is very important to many members of minority ethnic groups, usually more important than ethnic identity.
- There are variations, sometimes significant, both between and within religious organisations.

The significance of religion and religiosity in the contemporary world

This topic includes discussion of the nature and extent of secularisation in a global context and globalisation and the spread of religions. While the main focus of this topic is the UK, it is important to be able to place sociological discussions of religion and religiosity in a global context. Many of the issues facing the world are linked, to a greater or lesser extent, with religious ideologies. In the UK, undoubtedly now a multi-faith society, people on a daily basis come into contact with those holding diverse religious beliefs and, increasingly, with those of no religious beliefs.

In some parts of the world people of different faiths and no faith live and work alongside each other in relative harmony, while in other places people are persecuted for belonging to a particular religion. Religion is inextricably linked to politics and political action, sometimes with violent consequences. Whatever a person's beliefs, religion is something that cannot be ignored.

The nature and extent of secularisation

Secularisation: the concept

Secularisation is one of the most complex sociological concepts, and has been defined in many different ways.

Secularisation and the 'founding fathers'

Comte, Marx, Durkheim and Weber all argued that some degree of secularisation would be an inevitable outcome of **modernity**. Berger (1974) defined modernity as 'the growth and diffusion of a set of institutions rooted in the transformation of the economy by means of technology'.

Comte believed that as societies developed from the theological to the positivist stage, social behaviour would be directed by scientific, rational thought. As sociologists understood society, Comte believed that they would be able to bring about a new moral order based on scientific understanding, and sociology would become the new, secular, religion.

Marx believed that after the proletarian revolution there would be no need for religion, as the conditions that created religion, i.e. the existence of capitalism and the bourgeoisie, would disappear. In the new communist society there would be no need for people to seek comfort in the belief of a better life in the hereafter.

Durkheim also saw the role of religion changing as societies became more complex and mechanical solidarity was replaced by organic solidarity, where social cohesion is achieved by laws of contract rather than the shared norms and values arising out of religious beliefs and rituals.

Exam tip

Make sure in any discussion of secularisation that you make clear which definition(s) you are using.

Modernity In Europe usually refers to the period from the Enlightenment of the seventeenth century to the mid-twentieth century. It is where there is a decline in tradition and the development of a rational outlook on social issues, together with an attempt to shape social arrangements according to logical and scientific principles.

Knowledge check 25

What did Comte mean by 'the theological stage'?

Weber believed that the increasing rationality of complex industrial societies would lead to greater bureaucracy and centralised control, and there would be little room for belief in supernatural forces. He described this as 'the disenchantment' of the world.

The meaning of secularisation

Bryan Wilson

A commonly used definition is that of Wilson (1966), which is that secularisation is the process whereby religious thinking, practice and organisations lose their social significance. This definition has four parts. First, it describes a process, so this is something that takes place over time. This process then has three elements to it — thinking, practice and organisations. To explore the nature and extent of secularisation, then, we would have to look at each of these elements. Religious thinking and practice have sometimes been referred to as the 'three Bs' — believing, behaving and belonging. The final element is that of religious organisations — again, made complex by the increasing variety of religious groups in society. Another, and important, aspect of secularisation is to note exactly where we are looking. Many discussions are highly ethno-centric — they focus almost exclusively on Christianity, and in the Western world.

Larry Shiner

A more detailed analysis and overview of the concept was provided by Shiner (1967). He identified six definitions that underpinned the way that the concept of secularisation had been used:

- The decline of religion — this suggests that different aspects of religion will lose their social significance and will eventually disappear. This usage is similar to that of Wilson (above).
- Conformity with this world — as religions move their focus to worldly concerns and issues, the distinction between religion and other social institutions becomes weaker.
- Disengagement of society from religion — this is where religion ceases to provide the basis for understanding of the world and for action, and is increasingly relegated to the sphere of private spirituality. It has little or no influence on other institutions or on society in general.
- Transposition of religious beliefs and institutions — this is where institutions and beliefs that were once believed to be grounded in the divine sphere become seen as the results of individual and social thinking and behaviour.
- Desacrilisation of the world — this is where scientific or rational models are used to provide explanations that were once provided by religion, and where there is a declining place for mystery or the spiritual. This is similar to Weber's idea of 'disenchantment'.
- Movement from a sacred to a secular society — this is where people are accepting of social change, and religion is only one of a plurality of philosophies.

Knowledge check 26

Briefly explain what Durkheim meant by 'organic solidarity'.

Exam tip

If appropriate, it is useful to be able to refer to the fact that ideas about the decline of religion existed in the work of the 'founding fathers'. Their reasons and predictions differed, but they all predicted a decline in the importance of religion in the modern world.

Exam tip

This is a fairly long and complex list to learn, but it would be useful to show awareness of Shiner's attempt to analyse the different ways in which the concept has been defined and used.

Steve Bruce

For Bruce, secularisation is 'a long-term decline in the power, popularity and prestige of religious beliefs and rituals', which he claims is brought about by 'individualism, diversity and egalitarianism in the context of liberal democracy'.

Key concepts

secularisation; modernity; rationalisation; disenchantment; disengagement; desacrilisation

Evaluation

+ Without the concept of secularisation, it would be difficult to analyse and explain the undoubted changes that are taking place in religious belief and activity.
+ It is important to have clear definitions of secularisation because they determine how sociologists measure its nature and extent.
− The plurality of definitions makes it difficult to compare different accounts of the nature and extent of secularisation.
− Many discourses on secularisation are ethno-centric, looking only at Christianity in Western, developed societies.

Secularisation: believing

While one way of gauging the extent of people's belief is by what they do, such as how often they attend religious services, the most usual way, at least as far as the UK is concerned, is by looking at what they say. A number of surveys have looked at the extent to which people, regardless of their religious affiliation or practices, say that they believe in God, or a god, or a higher spiritual power. All surveys show a decline in the proportion of UK adults who say that they have such a belief.

A YouGov survey in 2015 found that a third (33%) of adults say they do not believe in God or a greater spiritual power of any kind. This is almost the same proportion (32%) who said that they believed in 'a god'. 20% said that they believed in 'a higher power', but not a god, while 14% said they did not know what they believed.

A ComRes poll carried out in 2012 for the Christian group Theos found that only 19% of respondents had 'a firm belief in God'. By this, they meant that these people agreed with the statement 'I know that God exists and I have no doubt about it'. By contrast, it was concluded from the data that 42% of respondents could be classified as atheists or agnostics. A Gallup poll conducted in 1963 found that only 14% fell into these categories. In the YouGov poll, 19% self-identified as atheists and 7% as agnostics.

As seen earlier, belief, or lack of it, varies with age. In the YouGov poll, only 25% of 18–24-year-olds believed in God or a higher spiritual power, while 40% had no belief at all in a god or higher spiritual power. Conversely, 41% of over-60s believed in God. The same poll showed that only 55% of those self-identifying as Christian actually

Knowledge check 27

Briefly explain the difference between an atheist and an agnostic.

believed in God, while 23% believed in 'some sort of greater spiritual power', though not a god, while 9% of self-identifying Christians said they didn't believe in any higher power.

The *European Values Study* carried out surveys into belief in different countries in 1981, 1991, 1998 and 2008, using the same question wording throughout. In the UK, those who said they did not believe in a god rose from 16% in 1981 to 33% in 2008.

The data indicate, then, a decline in religious belief in the UK, with smaller proportions claiming a belief in 'a god' and a growing number saying they have no belief in a God or any other spiritual power. There has also been an increase in those self-identifying as atheists or agnostics.

The Pew Research Center carried out an extensive survey of Muslims in 2011–12, covering 38,000 people in 39 countries. While the findings showed considerable variation between groups and countries on a range of issues, Muslims are generally united in the core tenets of their faith, with 88–100% saying they believed in God and revered the Prophet Mohammed.

As always, though, we have to be cautious where social surveys are concerned — they may have used different sampling methods, and the questions are likely to have been worded differently, either between different survey organisations or the same organisation over time.

David Voas (2003) is also sceptical of the data relating to those who state that they have a belief in God, saying that such professed beliefs were rarely acted upon. He said: 'We cannot conclude from the fact that people tell pollsters they believe in God that they give the matter any thought, find it significant, will feel the same next year or plan to do anything about it'.

One possible reason for the apparent discrepancy between those who say they are 'not religious' yet profess a belief in God or some kind of spiritual power is that the UK has officially established churches, and most people still consider Britain to be 'a Christian country'. This also helps to explain the gap between people who say that they are Christian, for example on the Census form, and the falling numbers of those who regularly attend religious services.

> **Exam tip**
>
> It is always useful to be able to refer to findings from different religions.

Key concepts

belief; God; higher spiritual power; atheist; agnostic

Evaluation

+ There is evidence that there is a declining belief in God or some other spiritual power.
+ The decline in belief appears stronger among younger people.
- Following trends over time is difficult as survey questions are not all the same.
- We have to take note of possible differences between people of different faiths.
- Some people may claim a belief in God or a spiritual power without this having any impact on their life.

Secularisation: behaving

By 'behaving', we are talking about religious practice — attending religious services, praying, following religious rules governing diet or dress, and so on. Some of the evidence is from quantitative data, such as church attendance statistics, but much is qualitative and based on what people say that they do. The main sources of information are statistics provided by the religious organisations themselves, including the Anglican, Catholic and Methodist groups, periodical church censuses, and data from large-scale surveys such as British Social Attitudes.

Attendance at worship

To put church attendance in context, in 1851 about half of the population in Britain attended church regularly. The figure is now around 8%.

One problem with survey data on this topic is that research has shown that people tend to exaggerate, or fail to recall accurately, how often they have attended religious services for purposes other than weddings, baptisms or funerals. McAndrew (2011) suggests an explanation for this: 'The exaggeration in surveys is thought to be less due to wanting to appear more religious in order to impress the survey interviewer (social desirability bias), and more due to respondents attempting to illustrate that they have a connection with churches and that this is an important part of their identity, even though they did not attend in the past week or month.'

The 2014 *British Social Attitudes* survey showed that 58.4% of the population said they never attended a religious service, and only 13% reported going to a service once a week or more. Catholics were the least likely to say that they never attended, while Anglicans were the most likely.

In terms of attendance at religious services, the Church of England is experiencing a steady decline. The BSA survey found that of the 16% of people who self-identified as belonging to the Church of England, more than half (51.9%) never attended a service and only 10% said they attended at least weekly. Statistics from 2013 showed that on a normal Sunday (i.e. not a special Christian day such as Easter or Christmas), the average urban Church of England had a congregation of 60, while in an average rural church the figure was just 19.

The Roman Catholic Church in the UK has had its congregations significantly boosted in some areas by the influx of devout young people from Poland. Overall, however, the Roman Catholic Church shows a similar pattern to many other churches and large denominations. Weekly attendance at mass in England and Wales fell by 30% between 1993 and 2010, accompanied by a fall in the Catholic population of more than 10%.

One group of UK churches not following the trend of falling congregations are the so-called 'black churches', whose congregations are largely people of Afro-Caribbean and African descent. Such churches are attracting ever-growing congregations, and it has been estimated that there are over half a million committed black Christians in the UK who attend worship on a frequent and regular basis. Most black churches are **Pentecostal** in nature.

There have also been some so-called 'mega-churches' opening in a few places in the UK, particularly London, such as the Australian-based Hillsong churches. To be

Knowledge check 28

Give an example of the type of data-collection source from which a sociologist might gain (a) quantitative and (b) qualitative data.

Pentecostalism A form of Christianity that emphasises the work of the Holy Spirit and believes that members should have direct experience of the presence of God. Services are energetic and dynamic, often with a strong focus on music and singing. Other features are 'speaking in tongues', faith healing and prophesying.

termed a mega-church, congregations should average at least 2,000 on a weekly basis. The Kingsway International Christian Centre, a London church led by a Nigerian pastor and with primarily West African members, recently located to Kent. It claims that 12,000 people regularly turn up to worship on a Sunday.

It is difficult to obtain figures for Muslim attendance at Friday prayers, but attendance at mosques seems to be high, particularly among men.

Praying and other activities

Using data from the 2008 British Social Attitudes survey, Clemence (2013) analysed activities other than attending religious services by people self-identifying as Anglican, Catholic or 'other Christian', which would include denominations and evangelical groups. Of those saying that they prayed once a week or more, the figures were 22.1% for Anglicans, 37.8% for Catholics and 41.4% for other Christians. Those in the 'other Christian' groups also showed a much greater propensity than Anglicans or Catholics to read the holy scriptures on a regular basis (23.7%) and take part in other church activities about once a month or more (24.3%).

Evaluation

+ The data appear consistent in showing that there has been a decline in many examples of religious behaviour, particularly attending services of worship.
+ There are important differences between different branches of faith.
+ The arrival of immigrants has had an impact on both traditional and newer forms of Christian worship.
− Particularly with some of the black evangelical churches, which may start as relatively informal groups meeting in people's homes, it is difficult to obtain figures for the number of worshippers.
− All data must be treated with caution, as there are significant possibilities of error.

Secularisation: belonging

In this context, 'belonging' refers to people's membership of various religious groups. This is a particularly difficult area for which to obtain even reasonably accurate statistics, particularly where membership of smaller groups, NRMs and New Age groups are concerned.

In addition, some churches cannot or do not collect membership statistics. As far as Christian churches are concerned, the Roman Catholic Church does not have 'members' — people are either 'part of the Catholic population' or 'Mass attenders'. The first gives an unrealistic view, so the usual measure of 'belonging' here is the number of people who attend Mass. Most New Churches and virtually all Pentecostal

Evangelical Christians Believe in living their life as far as possible in accordance with the New Testament gospels. They accept the Bible as the sole source of religious authority and believe that salvation is possible only by conversion and spiritual regeneration — being 'born again'.

groups count attendance only rather than any formal 'membership'. The Church of England uses the figures from its electoral roll, which are invariably higher than attendance numbers. Presbyterians, meanwhile, apply the notion of membership rigorously and can supply detailed figures. Baptist and Methodist membership figures are available from their head offices. The Salvation Army, Lutheran churches and Quakers can provide membership information, but the many overseas national churches, such as the Nigerian Redeemed Christian Church of God, have no membership figures and so provide attendance data only. Information about 'membership', then, can give only a very broad picture.

Looking at data on membership of UK churches from 1900, the peak year in terms of members was 1930, when there were 10.9 million members.

In 2010, the compilers of *Church Statistics*, figures published by the Church of England Archbishops' Council, sent a form to every Christian denomination in the UK for which a contact address was available, asking for figures on membership, attendance and the number of ministers for each year from 2005 to 2010 and with a forecast for 2015, with a reminder letter to those who had not replied to the original request. The numbers were then collated into ten broad denominational groups.

The data showed that membership/attendance (whichever figure was available) had declined by 6% in the five years 2005–10. Taking only those institutions that had more than 10,000 members in 2005, some of the sharpest declines were seen in the following:

- the Roman Catholic Church in Northern Ireland — minus 23%
- the Presbyterian Church of Wales — minus 20%
- the Church of Scotland — minus 25%
- the Methodist Church of Great Britain — minus 21%.

Those that had shown the largest growth included:

- the Redeemed Christian Church of God — plus 73%
- smaller Pentecostal churches — plus 27%
- Kingsway International Christian Centre — plus 20%
- the Seventh-Day Adventists — plus 17%.

Obviously, those in the latter list would have started from a smaller base than those in the former, but nevertheless, the overall picture is clear. *Church Statistics*, which compiled the data, reports that all those in the 'growth' list were evangelical and half of all those listed (in the full list) were black churches. Peter Brierley, an expert on church statistics, says that between 2008 and 2013, UK membership of Pentecostal churches grew by 25%, to almost half a million.

The so-called 'black churches', which are largely Pentecostalist, evangelical, charismatic and sometimes fundamentalist, are, in fact, the fastest-growing churches in the world. It is estimated that their membership in Britain is already around 1.7 million, which in terms of numbers puts them in third place behind the Anglican and Catholic churches.

In summary, then, the 'belonging' aspect of secularisation indicates that membership of established churches and denominations is falling, while there is considerable growth in membership of evangelical and Pentecostal churches, particularly those with primarily Afro-Caribbean and African congregations.

Exam tip

Even if you don't quote the actual examples of which groups can and cannot provide membership details, being able to explain the problems of gathering accurate data is important and will help to gain marks for evaluation.

Key concepts
membership; attendance

Evaluation
+ Membership/attendance figures indicate that secularisation is occurring, at least as far as the Christian faith is concerned.
+ The process is not, however, universal — some types of religious organisation are significantly increasing their membership, albeit from a relatively small base.
− The figures need to be treated with caution, as it is difficult to obtain accurate data.
− The data cover only larger and only Christian denominations — there are no accurate figures for membership of small NRMs and New Age groups, though these are likely to be very small.

Secularisation: religious organisations

In December 2015, the Commission on Religion and Belief in British Public Life published its report *Living with difference* after a 2-year consultation. It identified three key trends:

- the rise in the number of religious 'nones'
- the decline in Christianity, and within that faith the huge shift away from mainstream denominations to evangelical and Pentecostal churches
- the increased diversity of faith and the rapid demographic growth of the Muslim, Sikh and Hindu populations in the UK.

The report called for an overhaul of key areas of social life, including education, the law and the media, to reflect the reality of the UK in the twenty-first century. Among the recommendations, many of which would reduce the power of the Church of England as an institution, were the following:

- The coronation of the next monarch should change to reflect modern Britain. Currently, the monarch is crowned by the Archbishop of Canterbury and swears to uphold Protestantism and protect the Church of England, its bishops and its clergy.
- The 26 seats in the House of Lords currently held by Church of England bishops (the Lords Spiritual) should be reduced to allow representation of other faiths.
- The Charter of the BBC should continue to require the broadcaster to cover religion, but take into account Britain's changing religious landscape, giving voice to those speaking from a non-religious viewpoint, including humanism.
- In the light of widespread public dissatisfaction with media coverage of religion and belief, there should be better training for media professionals in this area.
- There should be far-reaching changes to the place of religion in schools, including the abolition of the legal requirement to hold daily acts of Christian worship in state schools. Selection on the basis of religion in faith schools should be curtailed, and the teaching of religion and belief in schools should be overhauled.

■ The Ministry of Justice should study the workings of religious tribunals and courts, such as Muslim Sharia and Jewish Beth Din courts, to disseminate best practice and promote gender equality.

The chair of the Commission, Dame Elizabeth Butler-Sloss, said the proposals in the report amounted to 'a new settlement for religion and belief in the UK' and were intended to provide 'space and a role for all within society, regardless of their beliefs or absence of them'.

It has yet to be seen how many of these recommendations will be implemented, and to what extent, but if they were, the power of some religious institutions in the UK would be significantly curtailed, while others would have a new role. Overall, the significance of the report is the recognition both of diverse faiths and the increase in those who have no faith.

Secularisation in the USA

The USA is often held up as an example that casts doubt on the idea that secularisation is occurring in the Western world. There are undoubtedly differences between the degree of religiosity in America and other Western nations.

For example, research by the Pew Research Center in its *Religious Landscape Study* of 2014, which sampled more than 35,000 American adults, indicated that religion was still very important in American life — 77% of American adults said that they are religiously affiliated, two-thirds pray every day and say that religion is important to their life, and 60% attend services at least once or twice a month. This is a very different picture from that found in Europe.

However, when the Pew Research Center compared the 2014 figures with those gathered for its previous *Religious Landscape Study*, which was in 2007, a slightly different picture emerged. The comparison showed that between 2007 and 2014:

■ the proportion of adults saying that they were religiously affiliated fell from 83% to 77%
■ those who said they were religiously unaffiliated rose from 16% to 23%
■ those who said they believed in God fell from 92% to 89%
■ those who self-identified as atheists rose from 1.6% to 3.1% and those self-identifying as agnostics rose from 2.4% to 4.0%.

There were also falls in the percentages of those who said they prayed daily, those who said religion was very important to their life, and those who said they attended a religious service at least monthly. A further finding was that younger Americans were less religious than their elders. Of the so-called Millennials (generally referring to those born after 1980), only 38% said that religion was important to them.

Nevertheless, and again in contrast with most European countries, 72% of Americans say they believe in heaven, which to them is a place 'where people who have lived good lives are eternally rewarded', and 58% of Americans say they believe in hell, which to them is a place 'where people who have led bad lives and die without being sorry are eternally punished'.

Thus, the overall picture from the USA shows that while levels of religiosity are considerably higher than in most European countries, the trend indicates that

> **Knowledge check 30**
>
> What is meant by 'humanism'?

> **Exam tip**
>
> There are lots of figures here, which are included to indicate to you the scale of what is happening. You are not expected to remember all the various percentages, but you do need to know what they indicate in terms of an overall situation or trend.

secularisation is beginning to occur. As younger Americans are less religious than their elders, it can be assumed that the process will continue.

Why is the USA different?

Both Wilson (1996) and Bruce (2013) put forward interesting hypotheses to explain the differences between religion in the USA and Europe. Wilson said that while Europeans secularised by abandoning their churches, Americans secularised their religion. Bruce's version of this idea was that secularisation has taken two forms. 'In Europe the churches became less popular; in the United States the churches became less religious.'

The suggestion here is that in America religion became, and continues to be, less about salvation and worship and more about personal fulfilment. American churches have also embraced many secular activities, developing their own radio and television stations and turning their churches more into community centres, running schools, play groups, therapy groups, gyms, etc. Many of them run their own publishing houses and sell books, CDs and DVDs. Bruce suggests that even the language has changed. 'Evil and sin have been turned into alienation and unhappiness.' He goes on to suggest that 'the purpose of religion is no longer to glorify God; it is to help find peace of mind and personal satisfaction'.

It is also suggested by some that the spread of secular ideas has been such that even religious conservatives defend traditional values with secular assumptions. For example, while many still believe that divorce is wrong, it is not because God forbids it but because it is dysfunctional for society. For those who think that abortion is wrong, the legal battles are fought on the secular principle that it infringes the right to life rather than on the grounds that it is inherently sinful. Research has shown that young evangelical Christians are far more accepting of gay marriage and abortion than their parents were. The Pew research of 2014 found that a small majority (54%) of American Christians now say that homosexuality should be accepted, rather than discouraged, by society, up from 44% in 2007.

Even among Mormons and evangelical Protestants, whose teachings say that homosexuality should be discouraged, over a third (36%) in both groups believe that it should be accepted.

Knowledge check 31

Briefly explain why the concept of 'secularisation' might not mean the same thing when applied to European and American populations.

Key concepts

secularisation; religious affiliation; religiosity; traditional values

Evaluation

+ Levels of belief and religiosity in the USA continue to be much higher than in European countries, casting some doubt on the secularisation thesis.
- Despite this, the trend suggests that Americans are becoming less religious in terms of believing, belonging and behaving.
- Many American churches and groups have adopted more secular ideas and patterns of behaviour, suggesting that in the USA, religion itself is becoming secular.

Globalisation and the spread of religions

The global picture

The UK is one of the least religious countries in the world. In a global ranking of 65 countries in 2015, the UK came six places from the bottom, with only 30% of the population saying that they were religious. This compares with 94% of people in Thailand and 93% of people in Armenia, Bangladesh, Georgia and Morocco who said that they were religious. At the bottom of the list were China (6%), Japan (13%) and Sweden (19%).

Research into religion worldwide in 2015 showed that globally, poorer nations tend to be more religious than wealthier nations. If we define poorer nations as those whose Gross Domestic Product (GDP) per capita is $10,000 or less, more than 80% of these populations say that religion is very important in their life. Such nations are found in sub-Saharan Africa, South America, Asia and the Pacific.

Conversely, if we look at richer nations, those whose GDP per capita is between $40,000 and $50,000, less than 30% of the populations say that religion is important to them. Such nations include Europe, Australia and Canada. A notable exception, however, is the USA, where GDP per capita is $60,000 and where 80% of the population say that religion is important to their life.

Despite this anomaly, on a global basis religiosity exists most strongly among vulnerable populations, especially in poorer nations where the people constantly face life-threatening risks.

The Pew-Templeton Global Religious Features Project looks at religion on a global basis. In 2010 its researchers analysed more than 2,500 censuses, surveys and population registers to look at religion on a country-by-country basis. Perhaps surprisingly, given the strength of the pro-secularisation debate in the West, they found that the world is an overwhelmingly religious place. More than eight out of ten of the world's people in that year identified with a religious group. 5.8 billion adults and children were religiously affiliated, comprising 84% of the world's population. This compared with roughly one in six (16%) who had no religious affiliation — though many of the religiously unaffiliated held some religious or spiritual belief.

The future of world religions

Based on the 2010 data and religious trends, the Pew Center looked at the projected changes in the world's major religions for the years 2010–50 and compared this with the projected growth in the world's population. These are its projections:

Growth in world's population 2010–50	35%
Muslims	73%
Christians	35%
Hindus	34%
Jews	16%
Folk religions	11%
Unaffiliated people	9%
Other religions	6%
Buddhists	-0.3%

Source: Pew Research Center [April 2015] *The Future of World Religions: Population Growth Projections 2010–2050.*

Knowledge check 32

Give one reason for the very low figure of those claiming to be religious in China.

Knowledge check 33

What do the initials GDP stand for?

Therefore the only religion with a predicted growth in excess of world population growth is Islam, and the only major religion predicted to show a slight decline in numbers is Buddhism.

Religion in Latin America

Worldwide, Pentecostalism has 300 million followers, including many in Africa and Latin America, and shows strong growth.

In recent decades, tens of millions of people in Latin America have left the Roman Catholic Church and converted to Pentecostal Christianity. Analysis of the reasons for this spectacular growth has shown some interesting findings.

One is to do with the message itself, which is known as 'prosperity theology', or the 'health and wealth gospel'. In essence, this teaches that faith and prayer can bring about significant improvement in people's lives and prosperity. Unlike the 'theodicy of disprivilege', which teaches that rewards will be in the afterlife, prosperity theology teaches that success can be gained in this life, a powerful draw for the poor and underprivileged.

Another aspect of Latin American Pentecostalism is the emphasis on faith healing, often by the laying on of hands. Many converts join the church at times of health crisis.

A further reason for the growth of Pentecostalism is that the preachers are the same kind of people as those in their flock — often unlettered, from the same area and ethnic group and speaking the same dialect as their congregations. Most Roman Catholic priests, meanwhile, are white and often from European backgrounds.

While initially the growth of Pentecostalism was largely among the poor, it is now spreading to middle-class professionals, who find appeal in the emphasis on 'inner healing', individual responsibility and prosperity.

A further group joining the converts are men who are struggling with alcohol and substance abuse. The Pentecostalist teachings promote a healthy lifestyle and offer help to those with addictions.

Islam

Events in Europe and elsewhere in the world have brought the Islamic faith to the forefront of much political, as well as religious, debate.

Muslims are the fastest-growing religious group in the world. In 2010, there were 1.6 billion Muslims globally, making up 23% of the world's population. While currently Islam is the second largest religion in the world, after Christianity, its significance is that it is the fastest-growing group. The Pew Research Center estimates that if current demographic trends continue, the number of Muslins will exceed the number of Christians by the end of this century.

Reasons for the growth of Islam

In effect, the main reason is a demographic one. Muslim women have a higher fertility rate than non-Muslims and the religiously non-affiliated Muslim women have, on average, 3.1 children, while the average for all other groups combined is 2.3. Another factor arising from the differential fertility rates is that Muslims are

Exam tip

Discussion of the decline in Catholicism and the growth of Pentecostalism in Latin America will enable you to show that there are differences within the broader Christian faith, which will help gain marks for analysis and evaluation in a debate about secularisation.

the youngest of all religious groups. Their median age in 2010 was 23, while for all non-Muslims it was 30. As far as Europe is concerned, the median age of Muslims in Europe in 2010 was 32, while for all other Europeans it was 40. The median age for the religiously unaffiliated, including atheists, agnostics and those with no particular religion, was 37, while for European Christians it was 42. These two factors combined — higher fertility rates and a younger population — will continue to have an effect on the relative size of Muslim and non-Muslim populations.

Muslims in Europe

In Europe in 2010, Cyprus and Bulgaria had the highest **proportion** of Muslims in their populations — 25.3% and 13.7% respectively. In terms of **numbers**, the largest Muslim populations in the EU were in Germany, France, the UK and Italy. However, many such statistics will have changed following the arrival of large numbers of Muslim refugees and asylum seekers throughout 2015. Whereas previous research showed generally favourable views of Muslims in most EU countries, tensions between Muslim and host populations have risen following terrorist attacks and threats by Daesh.

Religion and globalisation

The relationship between religion and globalisation is a complex one. One effect of globalisation is that ideas and information spread rapidly around the globe. It is thus easier for people to know about other cultures, including their religions. The growth of global political forums and transnational corporations has had an effect on religious organisations, many of which are now international with a global reach. Religious organisations have also benefited from the spread of global technologies, with developments such as websites and online sales of tracts and merchandise. One effect of globalisation, however, has been the growth of insecurity and mental stress, and many people have found hope and comfort in religion.

Negative effects have been seen in the rise of religious-based terrorism spreading beyond the country of origin, with groups such as Daesh and Boko Haram waging war in the name of their faith.

Secularisation: the global context

In the world as a whole, there are two distinct processes going on. In the majority of Western countries, there is considerable evidence that on almost all indices, people are becoming less religious and one could say with confidence that there is a strong case in favour of secularisation. Even in the USA, which is often held as an example against secularisation, many have pointed to the ways in which religion itself has taken on many secular features.

In many other parts of the world, however, religion is thriving and the case for secularisation is weak. In the late 1980s, Peter Berger, once a staunch believer in secularisation, said that he no longer believed in the secularisation thesis, as it could not explain the growth of radical Islam, fundamental and Pentecostal Christianity in Asia, Africa and Latin America, or the significant growth of evangelical mega-churches in the USA. These concerns were also shared by Rodney Stark.

Knowledge check 34

Explain briefly what is meant by the fertility rate.

Exam tip

When writing about secularisation, it is very important that you are clear about which parts of the world you are referring to. Being able to discuss the contrast between Europe and some other parts of the world will allow you to show the skills of analysis and evaluation. However, the focus of the question is likely to be on the UK and Europe, so keep your answer in proportion.

Key concepts

projected changes; Latin American Pentecostalism; prosperity theology; Islam; demography

Evaluation

+ With the exception of the USA, there is a link between wealth, poverty and the extent of secularisation.
+ It is predicted that almost all of the world's major religions will grow over the next 40 years.
+ Pentecostalist Christianity has shown strong growth in Latin America.
+ Islam in particular is predicted to show strong growth.
+ Some of the negative effects of globalisation on people's lives may increase the degree of religiosity.
- The apparent greater religiosity of the USA may mask a process of secularisation both within and outside the churches.
- The growth of Islam will be a result of demographic factors rather than more people converting to the faith.
- Political events may serve to increase tensions between Muslim and non-Muslim populations in Europe.

Summary

- When discussing secularisation, it is important to know which definition is being used.
- There is considerable evidence in Western countries that levels of religiosity are declining, particularly among younger people.
- In the UK, despite evidence that overall levels of secularisation are rising, some churches, particularly evangelical and Pentecostal groups with largely black membership, are growing.
- The USA appears to differ from other Western countries in that the population shows much higher levels of religiosity, but even here, there is evidence of a process of secularisation.
- Globally, religion remains very important to a high percentage of the world's population, with poorer countries showing much higher levels of religiosity than wealthier ones.
- Islam is the only world religion predicted to grow at a faster rate than the world's population over the next 40 years.

Questions & Answers

How to use this section

In this section you will find five test papers on the *Beliefs in society* topic. They are in the style of the questions that will be on A-level Paper 2 Section B. The first three have two student answers, one at about an A grade (Student A), the other at about a C grade (Student B), with comments throughout. Test papers 4 and 5 have the first two questions with student answers and comments, while the third question on each is for you to try yourself, although there are some tips to keep you on track.

You should read each question carefully and either try to answer it in full or at least make notes of how you would answer it *before* reading the student answers and comments. This might help you to pick up on mistakes you have made or things that you are doing well. Remember that there is no single perfect way of answering an exam question — the highest marks can be gained by taking different approaches, especially in the higher-mark questions. However, the comments should help to show you the kinds of approach that would do well, and some of the pitfalls to avoid.

As a general point, you should always read through the whole question before starting to write. When you come to answer the questions that are based on an Item, read the Item particularly carefully, as it will contain material that is essential to answering the question. Take care to show in your answer how you have used the material in the Item.

Examinable skills

AQA sociology examination papers are designed to test certain defined skills. These skills are expressed as assessment objectives (AOs) and are the same for AS and A-level, though the weighting given to each differs between the two levels. There are three AOs and it is important that you know what these are and what you have to be able to do in an exam to show your ability in each. Further guidance on each of the assessment objectives is given in the guidance and comments. In practice, many answers to questions, particularly those carrying the higher marks, will contain elements of all three AOs.

Assessment objective 1

Demonstrate knowledge and understanding of:
- **sociological theories, concepts and evidence**
- **sociological research methods.**

Your exam answers will have to demonstrate clearly to the examiners that your knowledge is accurate and appropriate to the topic being discussed and that you have a clear understanding of it. It is not enough simply to reproduce knowledge learned by rote; you must be able to use this knowledge in a meaningful way to answer the specific question set. This means that you must be able to *select* the appropriate knowledge from everything you know and use only the knowledge that is relevant to, and addresses the issues raised by, the question.

Assessment objective 2

Apply sociological theories, concepts, evidence and research methods to a range of issues.

In certain questions in the exam you will be presented with an Item — a short paragraph setting the context for the question that is to follow and providing you with some information to help answer it. You *must* take this relevant information and use (apply) it in your answer. However, 'applying' the material does not mean simply copying it from the Item and leaving it to speak for itself. You will need to show your understanding of the material by doing something with it, such as offering a criticism, explaining something about it, linking it to a particular sociological theory or offering another example of what is being stated or suggested. You will therefore be using your own knowledge to add to the information that you have been given and will be *applying* it appropriately to answer the question.

Assessment objective 3

Analyse and evaluate sociological theories, concepts, evidence and research methods in order to:
- **present arguments**
- **make judgements**
- **draw conclusions.**

The skill of *analysis* is shown by breaking something down into its component parts and subjecting them to detailed examination. Analysis is shown by providing answers (depending, of course, on what it is that you are analysing) to questions such as 'who said or who believes this?', 'what does this concept relate to?', 'what does this research method entail?', 'how was this evidence collected?' and so on. The skill of *evaluation* is shown by the ability to identify the strengths and weaknesses or limitations of any sociological material. It is not sufficient, however, simply to list the strengths or limitations of something — you need to be able to say *why* something is considered a strength or otherwise, and sometimes you will need to state *who* claims that this is a strength or weakness. Depending on what it is you are discussing, you may be able to reach a conclusion about the relative merits or otherwise of something, but remember that any conclusions should be based on the rational arguments and solid sociological evidence that you have presented during your answer.

Weighting of assessment objectives

In the exam papers, each AO is given a particular weighting, which indicates its relative importance to the overall mark gained. The weightings are not the same for AS and A-level, so be sure that you are aware of the one that is appropriate for the exam you will be taking.

Weighting for A-level examinations				
Assessment objective	Paper 1	Paper 2	Paper 3	Overall weighting
AO1	15	**13**	16	44
AO2	11	**11**	9	31
AO3	8	**9**	8	25
Overall	33 1/3	**33 1/3**	33 1/3	100

Command words

Ofqual, the body that sets the criteria for all GCE sociology specifications, has an approved list of 'command words' that are used in exam questions. The following are some of the most commonly used, but it is important to remember that the list is not exhaustive and occasionally other, similar, words or phrases may be used instead. All this shows how important it is to take time in an exam and read the questions very carefully before you start writing. It is worth learning what is meant by these command words, to ensure that you give an appropriate response.

- *Define* — give the meaning of something
- *Explain* — give purposes or reasons
- *Outline* — give the main characteristics
- *Outline and explain* — give the main characteristics and develop these
- *Using one example, briefly explain* — use an example to give a brief account of something
- *Analyse* — separate information into components and identify their characteristics
- *Evaluate* — make judgements from the available evidence
- *Applying material from the Item …* — draw on the material provided and develop it using your own knowledge to answer the question

■ The A-level examination

The topic of *Beliefs in society* is examined on Paper 2, Section B of the A-level examination, under option 4.2.5. The *full* exam for Paper 2 lasts for 2 hours and carries 80 marks, worth one-third of the total A-level marks. The *Beliefs in society* option carries 40 marks and is worth one-sixth of the total A-level mark. You will need to answer two 10-mark questions and one 20-mark question. You should spend about 1 hour on this option, dividing your time roughly into 10 minutes each on the first two 10-mark questions and about 25 minutes on the third, 20-mark question, giving you time to read the questions and Items carefully before you start writing and leaving some time to read through your answer at the end. Note that the numbering of the questions on these Test papers is the same as that which will appear on the exam paper, namely 13, 14 and 15.

Test paper 1

13 Outline and explain two ways in which religion can act as a force for change in society. (10 marks)

ⓔ It is a good idea to separate out the two ways, with either a bullet point for each or leaving a space between them. Remember that 'outline' means that you can be brief, and to 'explain' you will need to show exactly how, in your example, religion could (or did) bring about social change.

14 Read Item A and answer the question that follows.

> **Item A**
>
> On many counts of religiosity, women appear to be more religious than men. In the Christian faith, for example, women are more likely than men to attend religious services and to say that religion is important to their life. Some claim that this is because men and women move in different social spheres, so that men are more exposed than women to the influences of secularisation.

Applying material from Item A, analyse two explanations for the apparently greater religiosity of women compared with men. (10 marks)

ⓔ Remember that to analyse, you need to 'unpick' something to discuss its component parts. Here, you are given two ways in which the religiosity of women appears to differ from that of men, and one explanation that has been offered for this. You will need to think of a second. Note that the words 'appear to be' and 'apparently' are used. This should signal that you might be able to make an evaluative point here.

15 Read Item B and answer the question that follows.

> **Item B**
>
> New Religious Movements have emerged in many parts of the world and take many forms. Compared with the major world religions, their membership is small, though the problems of defining what is a New Religious Movement means that statistics have to be treated with caution. Some claim that people are drawn to such groups because many focus on current concerns, such as our relationship to the natural world and anxieties about the environment, while others argue that many New Religious Movements offer hope and comfort to those who feel socially marginalised and alienated from modern society.

Applying material from Item B and your knowledge, evaluate the view that membership of New Religious Movements is a response to social deprivation. (20 marks)

ⓔ You are given the important information that there are problems in defining what is a New Religious Movement — be sure to refer to this. You are also given two possible reasons for people joining NRMs. The focus of the question, however, is on the relationship between membership of NRMs and social deprivation, so don't lose sight of this. Remember that you are asked to 'evaluate' the view stated in the question, which means looking for possible strengths and weaknesses of the argument.

Student A

13 The association between religion and social change is particularly associated with Weber, who pointed out the ways in which the Calvinist version of Christianity provided favourable conditions for the development of modern capitalism.

ⓔ There is no need to write an introduction to this type of question. However, it can be helpful to show that you have located a statement within a particular perspective, though no additional marks are allocated for this. It is therefore important that if you choose to write an introduction, you keep your statement brief.

One way in which religion can act as a force for social change is when a group of religious leaders or believers acts to overthrow a regime which they think is corrupt or has strayed away from the 'true faith'. This was the case in Persia in 1978, when a group of Islamic clerics led by Ayatollah Khomeini moved against the government of the Shah. The Shah fled and Khomeini became the leader of the newly formed Islamic state of Iran. The new government overturned the Shah's liberal reforms and introduced a system of Islamic law. Education had to be based on Islamic teachings, women had to be veiled in public, and adulterers were to be stoned. In this case, the application of particular religious beliefs served to introduce a very different type of society.

ⓔ An appropriate example with good analysis. Note how the concluding sentence sums up what has gone before. This is a useful technique to develop for this type of question, providing it is kept short. When you are asked for 'two' somethings, it is a good idea to keep them quite separate. You can either do as here, starting each with 'One reason' (or example, or way, etc.) and then 'Another reason', or leave a space between them and use bullet points.

Another way in which religion can act as a force for change is when religious believers and leaders are prepared to campaign against social injustices. An example of this would be the civil rights movement in the USA in the 1950s and 1960s, which was closely linked with the black preacher Martin Luther King. At that time black Americans, particularly in the southern states, faced enormous discrimination in all spheres of life. King preached the Christian doctrine of non-violence and his followers and others took part in peaceful (on their part) demonstrations and marches, sometimes at considerable cost to themselves. In 1957 the clergy-led Southern Christian Leadership Conference was formed, with King as its head. Eventually the movement helped to bring about the 1964 Civil Rights Act, which outlawed segregation and discrimination on racial grounds. While not all participants in the civil rights movement were Christian believers, many of them were, and the Christian clergy provided the leadership that resulted in very important changes to American society.

ⓔ 10/10 marks awarded. Again, an appropriate example with good analysis. Note how the answer shows the link between religious beliefs and leadership and social change, which is summed up in the last paragraph.

Overall, the answer shows good knowledge and understanding of two examples of religion and social change. The material is relevant and well applied, with good analysis.

---

14 As stated in Item A, on many counts of religiosity, women appear to be more religious than men. As well as the examples stated in the Item, more women than men claim that they pray regularly.

ⓔ A brief and relevant introduction which refers directly to the Item but does not simply copy extracts from it.

> One explanation for the greater religiosity of women is referred to in the Item, namely that men and women move in different social spheres. What this means is that women are more likely than men to be largely confined to the domestic sphere, with the home and family as the main focus of their life. Men, on the other hand, are assumed to be the ones that work outside the home, and thus their lives are believed to have a wider focus. The suggestion is that if there is a movement in society towards a decline in personal faith and a move towards secularisation, which many would accept as happening, then men are likely to be exposed to these new ideas before women, and are therefore likely to become less religious than their wives or partners. Built into this is the idea of a 'time lag' — Bruce suggests that women will also become less religious, but this will take longer than it does for men. While the assumption about 'separate social spheres' might have been plausible in the 1950s and 1960s, it is hardly likely to apply today, where women are as likely as men to work outside the home and to be exposed to the same social ideas and influences as men. As an explanation for different levels of religiosity, this argument does not seem to be supported by the evidence.

ⓔ An appropriate reference to the Item, with further detail showing good understanding and analysis of the concept of 'different social spheres'. The final sentences show relevant evaluation. This student shows sufficient detail and skills to gain good marks, but does not write more than needed.

> Another example of why women are supposed to be more religious than men is based on the notion that men and women are 'programmed' differently. The suggestion is that women are more 'touchy-feely' than men, and that they respond more than men to anything to do with the emotions.

However, you can accept that there are differences without saying that these are built-in, or 'natural'. Despite many changes, males and females are still socialised differently, and girls are encouraged to relate more to their emotional side, while boys are encouraged to be more logical and outgoing. Women are, generally speaking, still responsible for the 'emotion work' in the family, and are often more involved with bringing up children and instilling moral values. They might therefore be more open to rituals and beliefs that have a focus on motherhood, the family and morality — as in the Christian religion, especially Roman Catholics with the 'cult of Mary'. One factor that suggests that it is socialisation and ideas about gender roles that are the most important factors, rather than innate biological differences, is that older women are more religious than younger ones, and the more that women's roles become similar to men's, the more the gender gap in religiosity disappears. Another factor against the 'natural' differences is that in many religions women are *not* more religious than men. This is perhaps why the question talks about women having 'apparently' greater religiosity than men.

e **10/10 marks awarded.** Again, some good analysis of another reason offered for women's greater religiosity. The answer also shows good knowledge and understanding, and there is an evaluative tone throughout. The last two sentences raise particularly important evaluative points.

Overall, the answer shows evidence of all three assessment skills and makes good and appropriate use of the Item. There is a range of relevant sociological concepts.

15 Weber introduced the idea of the 'theodicy of disprivilege', which said that some religious beliefs claimed that suffering in this world was a test of faith and part of God's plan, and all the worldly ills and deprivation would be put right in the next world. Such ideas were thought to be particularly attractive to those at the bottom of society, as they offered both an explanation for their hardships and lowly positions and also reassurance that their suffering would be rewarded in heaven. Such arguments were used to explain the attraction of Methodism to the working classes, but could equally be applied to later New Religious Movements (NRMs). As the Item states, NRMs which hold such beliefs might be argued to appeal to the socially marginalised and alienated.

e This introductory paragraph 'unpacks' the question by explaining why it is that some religious movements might appeal to the socially deprived. It shows good knowledge and understanding, and analyses the concept of the 'theodicy of disprivilege'.

However, the Item draws attention to two important points. One is that NRMs take many different forms, so there are problems of definition, and the other is that there are NRMs that draw members for reasons other than social disadvantage, such as environmental concerns.

e Two good points taken from the Item, showing how information can be used without simply copying out sections from the Item.

Taking first the point about different types of NRM, Wallis suggested that NRMs could be divided into three broad types. World-accommodating NRMs had beliefs and practices that allowed members to live 'normal' lives alongside their NRM membership. World-rejecting NRMs tended to be 'closed' groups who withdrew from the world and focused entirely on following the rules — sometimes bizarre ones — laid down by the leader of the group, usually a charismatic figure. These groups tended to have an 'us and them' mentality. The third group was 'world-affirming', that is, members were promised that membership of the NRM would help them to achieve worldly success, such as in business and personal relationships.

e A good summary of Wallis's typology.

Which, if any, of these types of group might appeal to the socially deprived and marginalised? It might be thought that world-affirming groups would have the most appeal, except that membership of such groups, such as Transcendental Meditation, the Alpha Course and Scientology, tends to be drawn from the middle classes, i.e. those who are already relatively (sometimes extremely) successful, such as celebrities Tom Cruise and John Travolta.

Some of the socially deprived might be attracted to world-rejecting groups, such as the Unification Church (Moonies). However, again, membership seems to be drawn primarily from the middle classes, and if the socially deprived saw their deprivation as a test of their faith, they would be more likely to continue to accept the status quo, rather than withdrawing from it, as they believe that their rewards would be in the afterlife. This leaves the world-accommodating groups, such as evangelicals and New Pentecostalists. These groups do indeed seem to draw those from lower in the social hierarchy, particularly those from minority ethnic groups, and their 'message' seems fairly close to Weber's idea of the theodicy of disprivilege.

It is useful to point out that some have challenged the idea of the attractiveness of the 'rewards in heaven' message to those at the bottom of the social scale, pointing out that working-class membership of the early Methodist movement was relatively low, and that many members of the working class were either hostile or indifferent to religion.

ⓔ A good examination of the three types of NRM according to Wallis, keeping a close focus on the question, using examples and showing good analysis and evaluation. An interesting evaluative point at the end.

> This leads to the second point taken from the Item, that there is no one type of NRM and that there are considerable differences between them. If we take the idea of environmental concerns as referred to in the Item and look at groups such as Gaia, again membership is highly skewed towards the middle classes. If we extend the idea of NRMs to include so-called New Age Movements, then the proportion of middle-class members tends to get even higher.

ⓔ Again, a relevant reference to the Item, and sticking with the idea raised in the question of possible links between NRMs and social deprivation.

> Stark and Bainbridge introduced the idea of 'rewards' and 'compensators'. Rewards are things that people desire and can gain more or less straight away, while compensators are things they are prepared to accept because the rewards offered are currently unattainable, such as having to wait for the afterlife. It may be that world-affirming and some New Age Movements offer immediate rewards, such as financial success or inner peace, so might prove attractive to middle-class people, while the socially deprived might focus more on compensators, so are attracted to religious movements that allow them to accept and come to terms with having a miserable life on Earth.

ⓔ An interesting point, again with a focus on why different social classes might be drawn to different types of NRM.

> In conclusion, it appears that *some* people who are marginalised and socially deprived might be led to join *some* type of NRM. However, many NRMs have such small membership that it is difficult to make generalisations about them. It is also very difficult to find out about membership and practices of world-rejecting NRMs, though Barker's work on the Moonies is interesting (and showed mainly middle-class membership). Finally, the wide variety of NRMs makes it impossible to make statements that would cover them all, and it is clear that many NRMs have a particular appeal for the middle classes rather than the socially deprived. Additionally, current trends suggest that an increasing number of people, including the socially deprived, are turning away from religion altogether and becoming secular in outlook.

ⓔ **20/20 marks awarded.** A good conclusion that draws on and summarises the previous discussion and is evaluative in tone. Overall, this shows detailed and accurate knowledge of a range of relevant material on the possible links between social disadvantage and membership of NRMs. There is a close focus on the question throughout, and both analysis and evaluation are explicit and relevant. Appropriate conclusions are drawn which do not simply repeat material but both summarise and develop it.

This is a particularly good answer, scoring full marks throughout. It is, of course, possible to gain an A grade without achieving full marks, but this is obviously something to aim for.

Overall mark: 40/40

Student B

13 Religion brought in social change when the Protestant beliefs helped to develop modern capitalism. Weber said that the Protestant ethic meant that people worked hard because work was a way of honouring God, but their Protestant beliefs did not allow conspicuous consumption so they saved their wealth and then invested it in their businesses. This provided the necessary capital.

e An appropriate example that could have been more developed. An accurate reference to Weber and appropriate use of the concepts of the Protestant ethic and conspicuous consumption, with some analysis. However, the last sentence is unclear — necessary capital for what?

In Poland some members of the Roman Catholic Church who were also union members supported the Solidarity movement against the Communist regime, receiving support from Pope John Paul II. This led eventually to semi-free elections and the formation of a Solidarity-led coalition government. The Catholic union leader Lech Walesa became president of Poland in 1990.

e **5/10 marks awarded.** An interesting example with good potential, but the link between religion and social change could have been explained more fully. There is little analysis.

14 As it says in the Item, women are more religious than men, being more likely than men to attend religious services and to say that religion is important in their life. As it also says in the Item, some people think that the reason for this is that men are more exposed than women to the influences of secularisation. The argument is that men and women have different roles, with the woman being the home maker and child rearer and the man the breadwinner. This does not really apply nowadays, though, as most women have jobs outside the home and men play a bigger part in domestic and childcare duties than earlier generations. This means that although there are still gender differences, men and women are broadly exposed to the same ideas, which would include secularisation.

e The first two sentences are mainly copied from the Item, which takes up valuable time and adds nothing to the argument. One important thing that could have been taken from the Item is the concept of 'different social spheres' — although the answer shows that this concept is understood, it would have been a good idea to make explicit reference to it. There is some analysis and evaluation of the argument, but the evaluation in the final sentence could have been made more explicit.

> Another thing that explains the difference between men and women is age. Britain is becoming a more secular society, and this is most noticeable in the younger age groups. Older people were brought up in a more religious age, where going to church and Sunday school were regular features of many people's lives. If you are not brought up in a religious household, you are less likely to be religious yourself. Most congregations in Christian churches, especially the mainstream ones, are composed of older people, and as women on average live longer than men, there are more older women than men in the population. Therefore it is not necessarily true that women are more religious than men.

e 6/10 marks awarded. This is a good example, with some analysis and basic evaluation. Differences within the Christian faith are hinted at ('especially the mainstream ones') but not developed — for example, many Pentecostal and evangelical churches have a younger membership with less marked gender differences, and it would have been useful to make reference to non-Christian faiths.

> **15** As it says in the Item, NRMs are found in many parts of the world, and even some of those found in the West are based on Eastern philosophies. Many people have had concerns about NRMs, as they feel that members are 'brainwashed' and may find it difficult to leave, even if they want to. Some groups have even led their members to commit suicide, such as the Heaven's Gate and People's Temple examples.

e A very brief reference to the Item, the relevance of which is not shown, followed by some material which, though accurate, is not related to the question. It is really important to make sure that you make best use of the time available by sticking closely to the set question.

> As it says in the Item, compared with the main world religions, NRM membership is small, and it is also not always clear what would count as an NRM. Eileen Barker and Roy Wallis think that we should use NRM rather than sect or cult as many people automatically think that sects and cults are dangerous organisations.
>
> The Item says that some NRMs offer hope and comfort to the socially marginalised and alienated. This is true in those cases where the message

of the NRM is that earthly suffering and misery is part of a divine plan, and that everything will be put right in the next world, as members will be 'saved' and will go to heaven. This, of course, applies to NRMs based on the Christian faith, which not all of them are.

e The first paragraph here is again not focused on the question, despite the reference to the Item. However, the next paragraph is more relevant, and there is a hint of evaluation at the end. It would have been helpful to give an example of a non-Christian-based NRM.

One reason why people at the bottom of society might be drawn to NRMs is that many of them offer practical help with day-to-day problems, such as running nurseries or food banks. Also, some NRMs such as smaller evangelical or Pentecostal groups are very inclusive, and help members to form strong social networks, which would help the socially marginalised and alienated feel that they were part of a group.

e Again, a focus on the question, with some suggestions regarding what some NRMs have to offer the socially deprived.

The Item says that people are drawn to NRMs because many focus on current concerns, such as our relationship to the natural world and anxieties about the environment. This would apply especially to so-called New Age groups. One example would be the Findhorn community, a small eco-village in Scotland whose residents focus on being environmentally friendly and finding inner spirituality. Most members of this kind of group come from the middle classes, so it is not social deprivation that attracts them. Findhorn has been in existence for over 50 years, which is unusual, as many NRMs are short-lived.

e Again, copying an unnecessarily long phrase from the Item, though the copied extract is then used in a relevant way. Findhorn provides a good and relevant example, which is linked to issues of the social background of members. The point about the duration of NRMs is an interesting one and could have been developed.

As there is no one type of NRM, it is not possible to say that people are drawn to NRMs because of any one particular thing. Some people who are at the bottom of society could well be drawn to NRMs that provide companionship and a promise of rewards in the afterlife, while others might be drawn to more world-rejecting groups, who could bolster people's self-esteem by showing them that they were part of a very exclusive group and that only they would be 'saved'. It seems though that world-rejecting groups are not as common as perhaps in the 1970s, and most people have to fit in their religion with their everyday lives.

ⓔ A relevant point is made in the first sentence, followed by some reasons why the socially deprived might join a particular kind of NRM, showing knowledge of two different types. A good evaluative point made in the last sentence, which could have been developed.

> Other people, mainly from the middle classes, who might have stressful jobs and busy lives, might be drawn to groups who claim to provide ways of dealing with stress and gaining inner peace, while others might have a strong focus on the environment.

ⓔ Potentially relevant, though not developed.

> In conclusion, the evidence does not show that membership of New Religious Movements is a response to social deprivation, though for some people it might be.

ⓔ **11/20 marks awarded.** A fairly weak conclusion, though it does refer to the question and is generally supported by the material used in the answer.

This answer shows broadly accurate knowledge largely related to the question but of limited range and depth. There is some analysis and evaluation, which remains undeveloped. Overall, this is a reasonably good response which has the potential to be improved by a stronger focus on the question and showing greater analysis and evaluation.

Overall mark: 22/40

Test paper 2

13 Outline and explain two differences between a church and a sect.   (10 marks)

ⓔ It sounds obvious, but take a moment to ensure that you have got the two correct religious organisations, namely church and sect, before you start writing. It is easy to make a mistake when faced with the pressure of an exam.

14 Read Item A and answer the question that follows.

Item A
Some sociologists believe that religious ideologies are used to manipulate or control believers so that they think and behave in certain ways that are beneficial to the interests of those in power. Althusser, for example, saw religion as part of the ideological state apparatus which served to prevent the majority of people from seeing what he considered to be their true class position.

Applying material from Item A, analyse two ways in which religious ideologies can be seen as serving the interests of a particular social group.   (10 marks)

ⓔ Remind yourself what is meant by an ideology before you start this. Remember to apply (use) the information in the Item, though you will also need to draw on your own knowledge.

15 Read Item B and answer the question that follows.

Item B

It is often claimed that Western societies are becoming increasingly secular. Those holding this view point to features such as the decline in attendance at religious services and the growing number of people who say that they have no religious affiliation. Critics of this view point out that in a postmodern world, religious beliefs and practices are changing, rather than disappearing, and religion still has an important role to play.

Applying material from Item B and your knowledge, evaluate the view that despite the apparent growth in secularisation, religion still performs important functions for society. (20 marks)

e The use of the word 'apparent' in the question will help you to make some evaluative points. It is worth jotting down some of the functions religion is claimed to perform for society before starting to write.

Student A

13 Weber defined a church as a large, well-established religious body. The phrase 'well-established' gives us one difference between a church and a sect. Churches have existed over sometimes long periods of time (such as the Roman Catholic Church) and often have developed close links with the state. For example, the Church of England has many formal links with the state, such as taking part in important ceremonies such as the coronation of the monarch, and also having a political role with bishops in the House of Lords, though its political role is much less than it was in medieval times. Sects, on the other hand, are frequently short-lived — or if they do continue over time they usually change their structure to become more formal, for example becoming a denomination. Sects tend to have no formal relations with the state — in fact, they are often in opposition to it and/or withdraw from the wider society.

e A good, clear explanation of one difference between a church and a sect. It would have been a good idea to include an example of a sect, perhaps one that became a denomination or one whose members withdrew from society. Giving an example can help in those cases where the explanation is not as clear as it might be, though that is not the case here.

Another difference between a church and a sect is that churches have a hierarchy of paid officials and membership is usually by ascription — people are born into the church through their parents' membership and are formally admitted through rituals such as infant baptism. Sects typically are led by a single charismatic leader, which is why many sects die out when this person dies. Membership usually takes place in adulthood.

e **7/10 marks awarded.** This is accurate, though the part on sects is rather brief. Again, an example of a sect led by a charismatic leader would have helped, as would a little more discussion on the effects of members joining as adults. For example, does the fact that sect members join voluntarily as adults mean that they are more committed to their beliefs than some of those who were enrolled in a church as infants? Two differences are given here (leadership and membership), which is not a problem, but there must be sufficient development of at least one to gain the marks.

Two relevant and accurate differences are identified and explained. There is some analysis, though some points could have been further developed, and it would have been helpful to include a few more examples.

---

14 An ideology is a set of ideas and beliefs which people use to make sense of their world. Religious ideologies are shared by many people (members of the same faith) who use them to guide and shape their behaviour and beliefs. Both Marx and Althusser believed that those in power used a particular religious ideology (Christianity) to make people think and behave in a way that benefited those in power, i.e. ruling members of the bourgeoisie. Examples of this would be the acceptance of the status quo in society as something ordained by God. Not only were the poor and members of the working class led to believe that it was God's will that they should be at the bottom of the social hierarchy, but that it was also God's will that those at the top should be there. A verse from a Christian hymn which is often used to sum this up talks about 'the rich man in his castle' and 'the poor man at his gate', going on to say 'God made them high and lowly and ordered their estate'. Given that this was originally published as a children's hymn, it could be used to show that the indoctrination (as some would see it) started early. The reason that this is important is that if the workers accepted their position in society as God-given, they would be much less likely to develop revolutionary ideas and try to make society more egalitarian. Equally, if the rich believed that their wealth was God's will, they would be less likely to feel guilty about it and try to share it with others.

ⓔ A good example, clearly explained and developed, with appropriate analysis. While the brief introduction is not necessary, it shows a clear understanding of the concept of ideology. While there is implicit use of the material in the Item, it would have been a good idea to make some explicit points, perhaps by referring to the 'ideological state apparatus' and people's 'true class position'.

Another way in which religious ideologies have been used to benefit a particular social group is liberation theology. This refers to a situation in South America in the 1960s and beyond where a group of Roman Catholics, including some priests and nuns, said that the church should fight against the poverty and ill-treatment of the poor. They argued that the Christian message was that the church should become a movement for those denied their true human rights, and that it was the duty of the church to bring about social change. The movement was not supported by the Pope, who said that it was trying to bring about a Marxist Utopia, and that the message was a distortion of Christianity. While it is difficult to say that liberation theology achieved its aims — after all, there is still extreme poverty in South America — it can be seen as an attempt to use religious ideology in the form of the Christian gospel to benefit (serve the interests of) a particular social group, in this case the poor rural peasantry. This is a case where ideology was not used to try to benefit those in power, as stated in the Item, but to try to serve the interests of those who lacked power.

e **9/10 marks awarded.** Another good example, with some analysis and evaluation and appropriate knowledge and understanding. The concluding sentences tie the answer in to the question asked, and there is a useful reference to the Item.

Overall, a sound answer showing appropriate skills.

15 Secularisation is usually defined as the process whereby religious thinking, practice and organisations lose their social significance. There is a lot of evidence that points to the fact that in most Western societies, including Britain, this process is occurring, and may even be accelerating.

e A good, brief introduction showing that the concept of secularisation is clearly understood, and also making a brief but relevant point about the situation in Britain.

Item B points out that there has been both a decline in church attendance and a growth in the number of religious 'nones', namely those that claim that they have no religious affiliation. In fact, there is also evidence that the third element of secularisation, the loss of the social significance of religious organisations, is also present.

With regard to church attendance, in 1851 about half the population in Britain regularly went to church on Sundays. Figures published in January 2016 showed that the number attending C of E services each week has fallen to below a million for the first time — now less than 2% of the population. A recent British Social Attitudes survey showed that well over half of people never go to a religious service, and just over one in ten goes at least once a week. Other forms of religious practice, such as praying and reading holy texts, have also shown evidence of decline.

e A good first paragraph which draws on (applies) material from the Item without simply copying it and then develops it, introducing the concept of religious 'nones'. The second paragraph provides supporting information about church attendance and other forms of religious behaviour.

With regard to religious belief, a YouGov survey from 2015 showed that just under a third of their sample said that they believed in God. About one in five said that they believed in some kind of 'higher power', while about a third said that they had no belief in a god or any spiritual power. This means that about half the population have some kind of spiritual belief, whether it is in God, a god, or some other kind of higher power. So some of the religious 'nones', while not affiliated, still have some kind of spiritual belief.

e More relevant knowledge, this time on religious belief. Note how you do not have to remember and quote precise percentages.

The religious organisation that traditionally exercises power in Britain, at least since Henry VIII's break from Rome, is the Church of England. While still playing an important role in ceremonies such as the coronation, and while still having 26 bishops in the House of Lords, the power of the C of E has declined significantly, and the recent report from the Commission on Religion in Public Life recommends that its power is diminished still further, to reflect the diverse pattern of belief and non-belief that exists in contemporary Britain.

e This is both accurate and relevant knowledge, but there is a danger that this student will not have left sufficient time to address the main thrust of the question, which is about not just secularisation but the possible functions religion still performs for society. It is essential that when writing to a time deadline, you keep the main focus on the set question.

However, the picture is not as clear-cut as some data suggest. While it is true that the C of E is in decline on a number of counts, some Christian churches are growing, particularly evangelical and Pentecostal churches with mainly black congregations. Congregations at some Roman Catholic churches have been considerably swelled by members of the growing Polish community in many parts of Britain. We must also remember the importance of other faiths, particularly Islam, Hinduism and Sikhism. Many from minority ethnic groups are very devout and the practice of their faith is very important to them. The USA provides an example of a society where religion and religious belief are still very strong.

e Some relevant knowledge and analysis casting some doubt on the extent of secularisation. It is important in this type of question not to focus simply on one type of church and one particular faith. The point about the USA could have been further explained and developed.

As Item B says, some critics of the secularisation thesis base their views on the fact that we live in a postmodern world, where many of the old certainties and religious practices are changing and where 'metanarratives' have lost their power. Some say that religion is now a 'pick and mix' affair, where people increasingly take elements from different forms of religion, choosing those that chime with their needs, beliefs and lifestyles.

This view is used to explain the growth of NRMs and particularly New Age practices. It is claimed that it is not possible to claim that Britain is becoming more secular just because fewer people attend weekly acts of worship or more people claim that they have no religious affiliation. Even among the religious 'nones', a considerable proportion say that they do believe in some kind of higher power or spiritual being, which we must surely accept as a form of religiosity.

e A good paragraph which picks up a point from the Item and develops it, showing some analysis and evaluation. It would have been helpful to explain the point about metanarratives.

So does religion still have an important role to play in society? Marxists, especially Althusser, would say that religion still performs the role in capitalist society of 'keeping the people in their place', and disguising their true class position. However, this argument is stronger if large sections of the population, especially the working class, are religious, and this seems less and less to be the case. If members of the working class are being 'kept down', it could be argued that this is more the result of government austerity measures than because of a belief that this is God's will.

Durkheim and the functionalists believe that religion is 'the moral glue' that binds society together, with its teaching of shared norms and values. This function is also difficult to accept in today's society, with different faiths teaching different values and many people with no religious beliefs at all. People in general seem to be turning away not only from conventional religion but also from political action — those in the working class are less likely to vote than the middle classes, and this is particularly true of the young.

e An evaluative paragraph looking at the possible role of religion in society from a Marxist and functionalist viewpoint, showing good knowledge and understanding.

> So — if it appears that religion does not have an important role for society as a whole, is it important for individuals? Here the answer appears to be 'yes', but for some people rather than all. Those who are practising members of the major religions in most cases will use their faith for comfort and strength in times of trouble and because of their belief in the afterlife. Those attracted to other kinds of beliefs again will have a particular motive — finding inner peace, helping to preserve the planet, being helped to achieve worldly success, etc. Many members of BME groups find that their religious beliefs and practices bring them joy and a sense of community.

e Another evaluative paragraph looking at the role of religion for individuals.

> In conclusion, while the extent of secularisation may not be quite as great as some claim, it does seem that the overall trend, at least for Britain and most Western societies, is towards greater secularisation. However, while the role of religion for society as a whole may be less important than in the past, it is undeniable that for some people religious faith and practice remain an important part of their life.

e **17/20 marks awarded.** A brief but relevant conclusion that addresses the set question and is supported by the preceding discussion.

A sound answer showing good knowledge of a range of relevant material and with some explicit analysis and evaluation. Good and appropriate use of the Item. There was perhaps slightly too much material on secularisation in the early part, rather than a more detailed discussion of the role of religion in postmodern society.

Overall, a good answer focused on the questions and showing relevant sociological knowledge and evidence of all three skills.

Overall mark: 33/40

Student B

13 A church usually has good relations with the state — some churches are the 'official' church for that country, such as the Church of England. Sects usually don't have this kind of formal recognition and may even be in opposition to the established church, such as the Dissenters who separated from the Church of England.

e A brief but accurate difference between a church and a sect, with an appropriate example of each.

A church will have a formal leader, such as the Archbishop of Canterbury or the Pope, who has usually 'come up through the ranks', while sect leaders are often charismatic figures who emerge almost from nowhere and attract members to the group. An example would be Marshall Applewhite, who founded the Heaven's Gate group, the so-called UFO cult.

ⓔ 6/10 marks awarded. Another appropriate difference, with examples, but not sufficiently developed and with only basic analysis.

14 One example would be the Taliban in Afghanistan, an Islamist fundamentalist group. They emerged during the Soviet occupation of Afghanistan and after the Soviets withdrew, promised to bring peace and security to the country and to introduce Islamic Sharia law. Although they were popular at first, they ruthlessly enforced their Islamic laws, saying that men had to wear beards and women wear the full veil, and stopping education for girls. The leaders used 'religious police' to enforce obedience to the law and keep themselves in power, trying to prevent any Western influences such as television and the internet from 'corrupting' the population.

ⓔ An interesting and unusual example, though with limited analysis.

Another example is the way in which some religious 'messages' are used to convince the population that everything in society comes from God, including your position in the social hierarchy. To stop those at the bottom trying to improve their position, they are told that it is their Christian duty to accept whatever position they are in, and to use their life to serve God by working hard. To sweeten this bitter pill, they are also assured that if they do this, there is a place reserved for them in Heaven and they will enjoy everlasting happiness. By accepting their lowly status and also working hard, they kept the ruling class in power without them having to use force. Althusser saw this as religion being part of the ideological state apparatus and preventing them seeing that it was capitalism, not God, that kept them at the bottom of society.

ⓔ 4/10 marks awarded. An appropriate example, though not always clear. There is some basic analysis and a belated though not direct reference to the Item right at the end. It is important to use (apply) material from the Item and to make explicit reference to it.

15 Item B says that some believe that Western societies are becoming more secular. Wilson says that secularisation is where religious beliefs, practices and organisations lose social significance. The Item says that there is evidence of secularisation because not as many people go to church and there are more people than ever saying that they do not belong to any religion.

e A good beginning, making appropriate reference to the Item and showing understanding of the concept of secularisation.

As well as the things mentioned in the Item, those saying that secularisation is happening also point out that not as many people as in the past say that they pray or that they believe in God, heaven and hell.

e Another reference to the Item, together with more examples of the process of secularisation.

On the other hand, we have to be careful not to jump to conclusions about secularisation. For a start, most of the evidence comes from Christianity and doesn't really take into account the growing number of Muslims, Hindus and Sikhs, who are often very religious. In some areas, the churches are almost empty while the mosques and temples are full. Even if we look at Christianity, some kinds of groups are growing, and there are even mega-churches in some places.

e An evaluative tone here, with some good points. It would have been better to have included examples of the kind of Christian group that is increasing in number, as well as an explanation of what a mega-church is.

The Item also says that not everybody agrees that secularisation is happening, and that in a postmodern world religious beliefs and practices are changing rather than disappearing. While many people are leaving the established religions, some are joining NRMs and New Age groups. The numbers are likely to be very small, but as many of these groups are informal, we don't actually know how many people are members. Steve Bruce says if you go into a bookshop you will find many shelves of books on things like Wicca, paganism, magic, using crystals for healing, etc. which seems to indicate that there is a fairly big market for these kinds of New Age beliefs — but can we say that these are religions? Some NRMs like Scientology claim to have millions of members worldwide, but this is difficult to prove, as in some ways the organisation is very secretive.

e Some interesting points, again with reference to material in the Item, and showing some analysis and evaluation.

> The Item says that religion still has an important role to play. I think that this depends on which religion and which country you are talking about. Obviously in some countries such as Iran, Iraq, Syria, Nigeria and Afghanistan, religion is very much tied up with politics, and you could therefore say that it does have an important role to play. This could also be said of the USA, where the New Christian Right are closely involved with the Republican Party. It seems as though religion in Britain is far less important than it used to be, though it is still an issue in Northern Ireland.

ⓔ **14/20 marks awarded.** Another appropriate reference to the Item and some potentially good examples, though the relevance of these could have been further explained. An evaluative point is made in the second sentence. The point about Northern Ireland, which is potentially relevant, is not explained.

Some good material here, generally focused on the question, and appropriate use of the Item. The relevance of some points is not drawn out and developed. There is evidence of accurate knowledge and understanding, and of both analysis and evaluation. Further discussion on some parts of the material would have increased the mark.

Overall, this answer has potential. A better focus and development in questions 13 and 14, and more evidence of the skills of analysis and evaluation, would have increased these marks, showing that it is important to do well in all parts of the question.

Overall mark: 24/40

Test paper 3

13 Outline and explain two problems with using church attendance statistics as a way of measuring the extent of secularisation. (10 marks)

ⓔ Make sure that you relate the problems of using church attendance statistics to the concept of secularisation.

14 Read Item A below and answer the question that follows.

> **Item A**
>
> While fundamentalism is often associated with Islam, there are fundamentalist groups in many other major religions, including Christianity. In the USA, for example, the so-called New Christian Right is a significant political force in some states, and its members have challenged many liberal reforms such as legislation on abortion. Some sociologists argue that fundamentalism is an inevitable reaction to the erosion of religious certainties in modern and postmodern societies.

Applying material from Item A, analyse two explanations for the rise in religious fundamentalism. (10 marks)

ⓔ The Item gives an example of the existence of fundamentalism in two different religions. Be sure to refer to this useful information.

15 Read Item B below and answer the question that follows.

The regular worshippers at most Christian churches are increasingly female. Since the Church of England voted to permit the ordination of women, and now has a female bishop, many women have expressed an interest in becoming ministers, and there are now more women than men in training for the ministry. It has been argued that the greater participation of women in many aspects of religious life has led to religion becoming 'gendered', which partly explains the growing absence of men at religious services.

Applying material from Item B and your own knowledge, evaluate the view that religion is becoming increasingly feminised.

(20 marks)

ⓔ This question gives you ample opportunity to show your knowledge of gender in different religious groups and faiths.

Student A

13 Secularisation refers to the declining importance of religion both for individuals and for society, and the proportion of people attending religious services is used as one indicator of this.

ⓔ While not essential, this type of brief introduction showing a clear understanding of the concept and the question is always helpful — though it does need to be brief.

The question talks about 'church attendance statistics', which is obviously a reference to the Christian religion. As a way of measuring the extent of secularisation, it is obviously not sufficient. The recent important report into Religion in Public Life emphasised many times that Britain is now a multi-faith society. Being able to show that attendance at Sunday worship for Christians is falling — which it is — is therefore showing only part of the picture.

ⓔ A relevant point, clearly expressed and with reference to an important report.

Islam, Hinduism, Judaism and Sikhism are also important faiths in Britain (in terms of numbers) so we would have to look at the picture in these faiths before being able to make statements about the extent of secularisation. This might prove problematic in that attendance statistics are not gathered in the same way for all faiths. It is difficult to find statistics for attendance at mosques in Britain, though evidence from Spain indicates that the longer a Muslim immigrant lives in a European country, the less likely s/he is to go regularly to a mosque. In addition to other major religions, some people are members of NRMs or New Age groups, for which few statistics are available, and many groups do not have any kind of formal act of worship, though their members might be religious — or at least have spiritual beliefs. So, using only Christian church attendance statistics is problematic when judging the extent of secularisation.

e Some good analysis and evaluation, still focused on the problem of using church attendance statistics and with relevant examples.

> A further problem arises if we take church attendance statistics themselves. There is no one single way that such statistics are collected, meaning that there must be very wide margins of error. There are two main ways. One is that the figures are supplied by the individual churches themselves. With some churches, especially in rural areas, suffering from sharp declines in attendance, there is the obvious temptation to inflate the figures, in case the diocese decides to close the church or combine several churches under one shared minister. Here is also the possible problem of double counting. If a person goes to mid-week as well as Sunday services, does that count as once or twice?

e A second problem is identified and clearly explained.

> The other way that attendance statistics are arrived at is by asking people if, and how often, they attend services. (Attendance at Christmas and Easter services, and at weddings and funerals, is usually excluded, as these occasions are unrepresentative when judging regular behaviour.) There are three main sources of potential error here. One is that people may exaggerate the number of times they go to church as they might feel guilty that they don't go often enough. The second is that they may genuinely forget the actual number and frequency. The third is that the sample might be unrepresentative, thus giving a skewed result. Therefore there is a problem with the actual attendance statistics themselves.

e **10/10 marks awarded.** Further accurate discussion of problems with church attendance statistics, showing good analysis and evaluation throughout.

This answer shows very good knowledge and understanding of the question and the material used in response to it. Relevant material is identified and accurately applied, and there is good analysis and evaluation throughout.

> **14** Religious fundamentalism refers to where there is a move to return to the original teachings of the faith. The Item mentions Islam as an example. Islamic fundamentalism came to the world's notice with the overthrow of the Shah of Persia and the creation of an Islamic state in the 1970s, but has spread far beyond Iran. The origin of this particular fundamentalism was a growing dissatisfaction with what the Islamic clerics saw as the creeping Westernisation of their society. It was felt that Islam had moved too far away from its core beliefs and, importantly, behaviour, and that a return to obedience to Sharia law was necessary to preserve the integrity of Islam. The war in Iraq also brought about a rise in Islamic fundamentalism as it was seen as a war against Islam itself. Islamic fundamentalism also exists in Nigeria,

in the form of Boko Haram, whose name roughly translates as 'Western education is forbidden'. These and other examples can be used to show that this form of fundamentalism is a reaction against what are seen as sinful and degenerate attributes of Western societies. Therefore, to a greater or lesser degree, such things are outlawed — such as education for girls, women going without the veil, the use of the internet and social media, Western films, music and television and so on. So in this case, Islamic fundamentalism, while it takes different forms, is mainly a reaction against Western ideas and practices rather than a move to a modern or postmodern society.

e The first sentence shows understanding of the concept of religious fundamentalism, and the example of Islam is taken from the Item. There are appropriate examples of Islamic fundamentalist groups and the final sentence is evaluative and directly addresses the set question. Some analysis and evaluation.

The Item also mentions Christian fundamentalism, using the example of the New Christian Right in America. This example is perhaps closer to linking fundamentalism to modern and postmodern society. The suggestion is that many of the tendencies of postmodern society strip away the old certainties and leave people feeling vulnerable and even confused. Examples of things that many members of Christian fundamentalist groups believe are undermining basic Christian values are the relaxing of laws on abortion, as mentioned in the Item, and also the acceptance of divorce, gay marriages and treating Sunday as just another day. There is the belief that sticking to 'the old ways' is the only true route to salvation. The reason that there is staunch support for the Republican Party among Christian fundamentalists is that it is by far the more conservative of the two main parties. Interestingly, it has been pointed out that although Christian fundamentalists are critical of many aspects of modern society, they actively embrace many aspects of it, such as the use of social media and the internet to spread their message.

e **8/10 marks awarded.** Good use of the Item and a focus on the set question. The possible link between postmodernism and fundamentalism could have been developed a little more

Overall, two appropriate explanations for the rise of religious fundamentalism are provided. The answer shows good knowledge and understanding.

15 Item B points out that the regular worshippers at most Christian churches are increasingly female. Firstly, is this true? With regard to most Anglican and Catholic churches, the answer is yes. A Tearfund Report showed that on average, Christian congregations were made up of 65% women. Secondly, what are the main reasons for this? There seem to be two main reasons. One is that religious worship is more common among older people in the population, and the increased longevity of women means that the older the population, the greater the proportion of women. The other reason seems to be that women are more attracted than men to the 'emotional' side of religion, such as taking part in rituals. Again, though, younger women are less likely to go to church, so the gender gap might lessen over time. Interestingly, even though the USA has higher levels of religiosity than Britain, the gender gap is evident here too.

e A good opening paragraph that takes a point from the Item and analyses and develops it. Some good evaluation. The final point, though interesting, is not developed — are the same trends evident in the USA?

The next points in the Item refer specifically to the Church of England. Since the ordination of women was permitted (though only after a long and bitter struggle), the number of women wishing to become ministers has greatly increased and about 20% of all ministers are women. Some claim that women are particularly attracted to the pastoral role of ministers — being a vicar is increasingly another way of being a carer and nurturer, traditionally female roles. In addition, ministers work unsociable hours and for relatively little pay — again, features associated with women's jobs. In the sense, then, that most worshippers are female, as are a growing number of ministers (in the Anglican Church), it could be argued that the church has a very strong female presence. Other Christian churches too show this trend (though women ministers are still not permitted in the Catholic Church). Evangelical and Pentecostal churches have around 16% female ministers, while for the Methodists the figure is about 40%. But does that mean that religion is being increasingly feminised? Although the Church of England now has a female bishop, it is difficult to imagine a time when the Archbishops of Canterbury and York are women, and there doesn't appear to be a move towards electing a female Pope. Most of the established Christian religions remain generally patriarchal in structure.

e Another analytical and evaluative paragraph, developing other material from the Item. An interesting point is made about women's 'caring' roles and why that may attract some of them to the ministry.

If we look at religions other than Christianity, though, we get a different picture. In other faiths, such as Islam and Judaism, the trends shown in many Christian churches are not apparent. With regard to Islam, while there are now some 1200 mosques and prayer rooms in the UK, 30% of them do not even have provision for women worshippers. In general, women do not become imams, and if they do lead Friday prayers, it is to female-only congregations. In Orthodox Jewry there are no female rabbis, and in the synagogue, men and women sit apart. Similarly, only boys can study the holy text and undertake the bar mitzvah ceremony. It is therefore difficult to say that in these cases religion is becoming feminised.

e An evaluative paragraph looking at religions other than Christianity to examine the issue of religion becoming feminised.

If we broaden our definition of 'religion' to include NRMs and New Age groups, an interesting picture emerges. Some of these groups seem to have a particular appeal for women, some claiming that they join such groups simply because they are less patriarchal and more welcoming to women than most established religions. Groups such as Wicca and Gaia seem to have a particular appeal for women, though Steve Bruce has pointed out that it is primarily middle-class women who have the time and money to engage with these movements.

e A further brief discussion of how membership of some groups is a reaction against the presumed patriarchy of established religion.

However, in the light of increasing secularisation and declining church attendance in general, some concern has been expressed over the small proportion of men who are regular worshippers. Some American churches have argued that the greater number of women in the congregation and doing all the things that keep a church running means that churches have lost their appeal for men — in short, they are not 'masculine' enough. Some churches in Alaska have renamed their Sunday schools as 'Adventure Land' and introduced more physical activities and commercially produced DVDs to attract young boys, in the hope that they will become regular worshippers as they grow older. Others suggest that pastors build their sermons around 'manly' things that will appeal to men, such as bringing an interesting object into the pulpit and weaving a Christian message around that. While these are interesting approaches, it is difficult to see how they would make a huge difference overall. You could argue that if having women ministers and largely female congregations puts men off, then the problem is not so much with religion as with society's patriarchal attitudes. Closer to home, Helen Coffey, writing in the *Daily Telegraph*, suggested that the church would attract more men if it were seen to be relevant to their life and to society in general. She pointed out the Church of England recently severed its links with the payday lender Wonga after the Archbishop of Canterbury, Justin Welby, criticised Wonga for pushing already poor people further into debt. The C of E is also in the process of setting up credit unions to help poorer people obtain credit. The Archbishop has also criticised the government for the rise in people needing to use food banks as a result of austerity measures, and several churches now run their own food banks for members of the local community, not just church members.

ⓔ A detailed paragraph taking a wider look at gendered religion, showing good knowledge and understanding, with some analysis and evaluation. An interesting point is made about society's patriarchal attitudes which is linked to the issue of reasons for the lack of male worshippers.

In conclusion, it seems that it would be fair to say that many Christian churches and denominations are becoming 'feminised', if by that we mean that there are more female worshippers and a growing number of female ministers. However, in terms of overall leadership, these churches remain male-dominated and therefore arguably patriarchal in structure. Also, if we look at other religions, the male–female ratio is more equal or even reversed. Overall, then, it is not true that religion is becoming increasingly feminised.

ⓔ 18/20 marks awarded. A succinct and appropriate conclusion that arises out of the material presented and answers the set question.

Overall, this is a sound answer that shows broad and relevant knowledge and understanding and addresses the set questions. There is a generally analytical and evaluative approach. Appropriate use is made of the Items.

Overall mark: 36/40

Student B

13 One problem with using church attendance statistics to measure secularisation is that they are probably not accurate. If vicars and priests are asked to say how many people attend their services, they are likely to over-estimate so as not to look as though they aren't doing enough to attract worshippers. Even if their figures are correct, there is the problem of double-counting, as some people might go to church more than once a week. If you take all services through the week, then you can get double-counting, but if you only take Sundays, you will miss people who go in the week but can't make it at weekends.

ⓔ The problem of the unreliability of attendance statistics reported by ministers is identified and explained.

> Another problem is that attendance at church is only one way of being religious. Some people may have strong religious feelings but not go to church. This may be because their work patterns make it difficult, they may be too infirm to leave the house or they may belong to a group that does not even have regular acts of worship. Some people prefer to have informal religious prayer meetings in their home, where they study the Bible, or even watch *Songs of Praise* on television and join in that way.

(e) **6/10 marks awarded.** Another problem identified and explained. Reasonably good knowledge and understanding of relevant material shown in this answer, with some basic analysis.

> **14** As the Item says, the New Christian Right is an example of religious fundamentalism. Some people in these groups claim that the Bible is literally true, so they believe that God created the world in seven days and therefore teach creationism in schools rather than evolution. They are also against things such as legalised abortion and homosexuality, saying that homosexuality is a disease that can be cured. The reason they hold these beliefs is that they point to things in the Bible that say that they are forbidden or sinful. The main reason that this movement has grown is that they have been very successful in using technologies to spread their message, from the so-called 'televangelists' of the 1970s and now with their own radio and television stations and use of social media and the internet.

(e) A brief reference to the Item followed by a discussion of the New Christian Right. While the material is accurate, there is no clear understanding shown of what religious fundamentalism actually is, though there is implicit understanding with the reference to the literal interpretation of the Bible. The last sentence, while offering a reason for the growth in members of the NCR, does not link this to the growth in religious fundamentalism *per se*.

> Another religion associated with fundamentalism is Islam, as mentioned in the Item. There are several Islamic fundamentalist groups, in different countries, but they all seem to want to halt the spread of modern influences, especially those from the West. They believe in a very strict interpretation of the Quran and want a return to Sharia law. As the Item says, one reason for the rise of fundamentalism is a reaction to the forces of modernity and postmodernity. Islamic religious leaders appear to feel threatened by Western influences, and are able to persuade many young men (and women) that they should fight a 'holy war' against Western societies, often with violent results, such as the recent attacks in Paris. It could be argued that this type of fundamentalism is as much political as purely religious.

ⓔ 4/10 marks awarded. Another couple of references to the Item. There is some relevant knowledge about Islam linked to fundamentalism, but some of the material is only implicitly linked to the set question. There is some basic analysis, and a potentially interesting point is made in the final sentence but not developed.

15 As the Item points out, most people in the congregations of Christian churches are increasingly female. Not only are they female, they are increasingly older. As Bruce said, elderly women are now the 'key carriers of religion', along with members of minority ethnic groups. Not only are women in the majority at services, they are also very involved in the day-to-day running of many churches, giving up their time for activities such as cleaning, doing the flowers, running Sunday schools and organising fund-raising activities.

ⓔ A good start, with a relevant reference to the Item which is then appropriately developed.

It is also true that it is increasingly likely that a church minister will be a woman, who now make up about 20% of Church of England ministers. Since the first female ministers were ordained, a growing number of women have either trained or are in training for the ministry, as it says in the Item. With the appointment of the first C of E female bishop, this trend seems likely to continue.

ⓔ Another reference to the Item, with some development.

Let us take the first point, about the male/female ratio in congregations. The main factor here is a demographic one. Women live longer than men, women have historically outnumbered men as far as going to church is concerned, so it is not surprising that as the average age of congregations rises, you will find more women than men. As fewer younger people have a religious affiliation, so the average age of those who do go to church will continue to rise. With the difference in life expectancy already mentioned, the older the congregation, the more it will be dominated by females. Therefore this is a demographic issue, not purely a religious one.

ⓔ A good evaluative paragraph focused on the question.

So, if by religion becoming 'gendered' we mean that there are more women than men involved in religious activities, why should this in itself explain the relative lack of men? Is the suggestion that religion is becoming seen as a 'female' thing, such as certain jobs are? If so, we should ask ourselves why the presence of a majority of women should put men off. Some have suggested that churches should look for ways of making religion more 'manly', but this seems to sidestep the issue.

ⓔ Some interesting points raised about gender and religion.

> But is it really true that religion is gendered? The answer really is 'no'. Firstly, even within Christianity the leaders of the religious bodies are almost entirely male. If we look at other religions, such as Islam and Judaism, these are clearly male-dominated in a number of ways.

ⓔ Some interesting points that need further explanation and development.

> Secondly, we should bear in mind that even among many Muslims and Jews, the younger generations are less religious than their elders. This tendency is particularly strong in the Christian faith. This means that over time there will not simply be an absence of men at acts of religious worship, but of people of both sexes.

ⓔ Another relevant point.

> So, to answer the point about religion becoming increasingly feminised, the answer overall appears to be no. In most Christian congregations, female worshippers outnumber males, but this is explained mainly by demographics. The number of women ministers is increasing, but they are still well in the minority. It is not just men staying away from acts of worship, but younger people of both sexes. Most religions other than Christianity are still overwhelmingly 'masculine' on most counts.

ⓔ 15/20 marks awarded. A brief but relevant conclusion that provides an answer to the set question. The material presented is accurate and relevant to the question, though not always fully developed. There is some explicit analysis and evaluation.

Overall, a generally competent answer, let down by the response to question 14. There is evidence that most of the questions are understood and most material presented attempts to address them. Reasonably good analysis and evaluation.

Overall mark: 25/40

Test paper 4

13 Outline and explain two possible reasons for the growth in New Religious Movements.

(10 marks)

ⓔ You may find it helpful to include a one-sentence definition of a New Religious Movement. Explanations could include features of postmodern society and the growth of 'new' concerns such as the protection of the environment. Remember that NRMs take many different forms.

14 Read Item A below and answer the question that follows.

Item A

One view of religion sees it as a unifying force, binding individuals together and integrating them into the values of their society. An opposing view sees religion as essentially based on conflict, helping to maintain an unequal society and preventing those at the bottom from seeing their true class position.

Applying material from Item A, analyse two differences between functionalist and Marxist views of the role of religion in society. (10 marks)

ⓔ When using the Item, be sure to make it clear that you understand which sentence reflects which of the two views. You will need to find a further difference between the two views.

Student A

13 'New Religious Movement' is the name given by sociologists to religious groups other than churches and denominations — groups that were often referred to as sects or cults. The term covers many different types of organisation, and there has been a growth in the past 50 years or so.

ⓔ While not necessary, a brief introduction such as this, showing a clear understanding of the concept in question, is often helpful.

One possible reason for the growth in NRMs is a response to significant and rapid social change. The social, political and economic changes brought about as a result of late modernity and postmodernity have caused some people to feel lost as the old certainties of class, work and community have been eroded or even disappeared. The established churches seem to many to be unable or unwilling to help people cope with these changes, so instead many have turned to some kind of NRM that offers them a sense of meaning in their life, moral guidance and a sense of security, as the metanarrative that was established religion seems to have failed to live up to its promise. Sociologists such as Wilson have noted that NRMs often appear in times of rapid social change. While some people might turn to the world-rejecting NRMs and withdraw from the wider society, many people affected by social change will be drawn to world-accommodating or world-affirming groups, as these seem more in tune with modern life.

ⓔ One suitable reason offered and explained, with some analysis and good use of appropriate concepts. It might have been helpful to give a very brief explanation of what is meant by world-accommodating and world-affirming groups, or an example of each. A good technique, shown here, is to clearly state your reason (or explanation, or whatever) in the first sentence and then spend the rest of the time developing it.

A second possible reason is relative deprivation. While Weber and Troeltsch suggested that sects had an appeal to the deprived and marginalised groups in society, promising them future rewards and explanations for their worldly sufferings, Stark and Bainbridge suggest that more recently, people may be drawn to NRMs because of feelings of relative deprivation. That is, they are not deprived in the sense of being in poverty or being at the very bottom of society, but they can see that their lives aren't as fulfilling as they might be. They feel spiritually deprived and look for something to give their life meaning. Others may feel that they are deprived in terms of material success, so might be drawn to NRMs that claim to help with achieving success at work. Particularly in the USA, there has been a growth in NRMs such as Scientology, Transcendental Meditation and Human Potential.

ⓔ **9/10 marks awarded.** A second appropriate reason offered and explained, with some analysis and relevant examples. Good knowledge and understanding shown throughout the answer. Material from the Item is well applied.

14 The first view expressed in Item A reflects the functionalist view of religion, developed by Durkheim, but also expressed in the writings of Malinowski and Parsons.

ⓔ A good start that correctly identifies the view in the Item and mentions some sociologists holding this view.

As stated in the Item, functionalists view religion as an integrating force, binding individuals together. The main way that this happens is through the moral guidance offered by religion and the shared rituals associated with any form of religious worship. Durkheim believed that in worshipping the sacred objects of a religion, members were actually worshipping society itself. By people coming together in shared rituals, Durkheim believed that the shared values of that society would be both expressed and reinforced, resulting in social solidarity and the reduction of conflict. While religion in complex societies was obviously different in form, Durkheim believed that it still performed the same integrating function.

ⓔ A brief but accurate account of how functionalists believe that religion serves

The Marxist view of religion, as expressed in the Item, is that it is essentially based on the conflict of one class against another. Religion is seen as part of what Althusser called the 'ideological state apparatus', this being the institutions of society that act to prevent the members of the working class from seeing their true class position as exploited wage labourers. Thus, far from binding all members of society into a unified group, religion serves to blind one group as to what Marxists believe is its true class position, and protects and defends the interests of just one group, namely the bourgeoisie, or ruling class.

e This picks out the main points of the Marxist view of religion, focusing on the difference between functionalism and Marxism with regard to integration versus conflict as expressed in the Item.

A second difference between functionalist and Marxist views of religion is that functionalists believe that religion is good (functional) for both individuals and society as a whole. Society benefits in that religion passes on and reinforces shared moral values, thus reducing conflict, while individuals benefit from a feeling of belonging to their society and having a belief system that explains natural phenomena and offers comfort for life's darker moments, such as death and disasters.

e The second point addresses the 'functional' aspect of religion.

Marxists, however, do not see religion as being functional for society at all. Those who benefit from religion are members of the bourgeoisie, while religion is highly dysfunctional for the proletariat. This is because religion reinforces a highly unequal society by justifying these inequalities as the result of divine will. Religion is thus highly detrimental to the interests of the proletariat. However, some neo-Marxists accept that under certain conditions religion can act in the interests of the poor and oppressed, as with liberation theology. With regard to individuals, Marx saw that in a capitalist society, religion could in one way be functional for individuals, in that its message could bring comfort to people whose lives were marked by poverty and deprivation. He referred to religion as 'the opium of the people' and 'the heart of a heartless world', recognising that it could dull the pain of exploitation. However, in another sense, religion was not functional for members of the proletariat as it kept them in a passive and fatalistic, rather than a revolutionary, state so that they would not rise up and overthrow the system that brought about their misery and exploitation.

e **10/10 marks awarded.** A clear explanation of how Marxists differ from functionalists on the benefits of religion to society, with an interesting point about neo-Marxist views. There is acknowledgement that both functionalism and Marxism accept that religion can help individuals to cope with misery, though this point is developed to show where there are differences. A good answer showing understanding of the question and the response to it, with appropriate analysis.

Student B

13 One type of NRM is New Age Movements and these have grown rapidly. One explanation is that many people have become dissatisfied with modern-day consumer culture and feel that the world has become too materialistic. They are looking for a more spiritual dimension to their life and are drawn to movements that seem to offer this. One type of movement promises to show people a way to live in harmony as a community, such as the Findhorn Project. This is a kind of commune, and has been going for over 50 years, though only a relatively small number of people are living there at any one time. One problem with this is that not everybody is either willing or able to up sticks and move away from family and conventional work.

Another type of New Age Movement are client cults, so called because they offer 'services' to members such as healing, aromatherapy, massage, etc. Some people have said that postmodern society is a 'pick 'n' mix' society where people will take what they think is best for their needs and wants, so people might belong to more than one group, taking something different from each one. Bruce has pointed out that the membership of this type of group is typically middle-class and mainly female — middle-class because these people have the time and money to spend, and female because many of the practices such as healing, aromatherapy, etc. are traditionally more appealing to females than to males.

ⓔ This focuses on one type of NRM and offers a suitable explanation for its growth. There is appropriate knowledge and understanding, some relevant examples and some analysis.

Another reason is deprivation. This kind of NRM is attractive to people who are marginalised and at the bottom of society. Globalisation has increased the number of people in the world who are in poverty, many of them in societies where upward social mobility is difficult or impossible. They will be drawn to NRMs that offer hope and comfort and help to cope with their situation. This helps to explain the growth of Pentecostalism in large parts of Africa and South America. While not many people here live in that kind of poverty, some members of BME groups are also drawn to this kind of movement.

ⓔ 6/10 marks awarded. An interesting example in that it looks at NRMs in a global context as well as in the UK. There is a relevant example and some basic analysis. This part of the answer would have benefited from a little more discussion of what Pentecostalism offers and some reasons why some BME groups in the UK would also be drawn to this type of NRM. This is basically sound but lacking in detail.

14 As said in the Item, functionalists see religion as a unifying force, binding individuals together and integrating them into the values of their society. Durkheim developed these views by studying 'primitive' religions in simple societies such as Aborigines. He looked at people worshipping sacred objects such as totem poles and said that these represented the values of that society, so that people were really worshipping society itself. As they came together in acts of worship, they were made to feel that they were part of the society.

e Copying longer extracts from the Item is not usually a good idea and wastes time. Learn to take the essential points from the Item and develop them, rather than simply repeating them. A brief but accurate summary of Durkheim's views on religion in simple societies. A reference to the role of religion in industrial societies would have been useful here.

Marxists, on the other hand, see religion as based on conflict, namely bourgeoisie versus proletariat. Religion acts in the interests of the ruling class (bourgeoisie) by keeping the proletariat in their place. This is done by the main message of religion, that God has decided what everybody's place in society should be and they should accept it. When members of the proletariat accept this view, they turn away from revolution and attempts to bring about a more equal society. So although there is not very often real conflict between the classes, religion hides the underlying conflict of interest between them.

e The Marxist view on religion as based on conflict is stated. Some basic analysis, and no direct reference to the Item.

Another difference between functionalists and Marxists is that functionalists see religion as being good for people. It teaches them a moral code that helps them to integrate into society and live peacefully with others. It also gives comfort in times of hardship and provides rituals for the main life events of birth and death. Marxists also say that religion can comfort people, but they believe that it is dysfunctional for the working class as although they may be comforted, they are still exploited.

e 5/10 marks awarded. Basically accurate, but very brief. Reasonable knowledge and understanding of the question and the material offered in response and some basic analysis, but overall the answer lacks development.

Practice question

15 Read Item B and answer the question that follows.

Item B

Many members of minority ethnic groups practise a religion that is different from the major religion of the host society. The religious and cultural rituals and traditions of their religion not only offer comfort but are very important to the way they lead their lives, enabling them to maintain a distinct religious identity.

Applying material from Item B and your knowledge, evaluate the view that the religious beliefs and practices of many members of minority ethnic groups constitute the most important part of their identity. (20 marks)

ⓔ The material in the Content section on religion and ethnicity (see pp. 32–34) will provide useful material when answering this. Try to include more than one religion in your discussion.

Test paper 5

13 **Outline and explain two ways in which religion can act as a source of conflict in society.** (10 marks)

ⓔ Remember that conflict can occur within, as well as between, religions.

14 Read Item A and answer the question that follows.

Item A

From the late 1960s, many Western societies saw a growth in the number of New Religious Movements, particularly sects. Concerns were raised about the number of young people cutting ties with their families and friends to join sects with charismatic leaders. Some sects seemed to be particularly successful, claiming that they had thousands of members.

Applying material from Item A, analyse two problems of measuring the extent of sect membership in society. (10 marks)

ⓔ Remember to keep the focus on sects rather than on other types of NRM, and on the problems of measuring membership. Different types of sect might pose different problems of measurement.

Student A

13 One way in which religion can act as a source of conflict is when members of two different religions hold such strong views that they are prepared to take action against members of the other religion. Actions can be those of members of one group physically attacking the people (and sometimes property) belonging to the other religion, or can be those of governments, for example placing restrictions on those wishing to follow a minority religion. There are many examples of this in different parts of the world. These include conflicts between Jews and Muslims in Israel, between Hindus and Muslims in Pakistan and between Muslims and Coptic Christians in Egypt.

ⓔ A clear account of one source of religious conflict, with good examples.

However, Alan Aldridge points out that conflicts are likely to occur where religious divisions coincide with political and social divisions. This would explain the position of Christians in China, where the ruling Communist Party is officially atheist, and where there are many restrictions on Christians, and even claims of human rights abuses. Christianity is seen as a subversive religion, with its followers open to foreign (Western) influences, which the ruling party is very much against. Similarly, the Dalits (untouchables) in India, below even the lowest group in the caste system, are still victimised and have restricted access to education and thus certain jobs, despite the fact that officially the caste system has been abolished. These types of religious conflict stem from a high level of intolerance on the part of one group, who may feel threatened by the existence of the other group, and obviously go against Durkheim's view of religion as a source of social cohesion.

ⓔ An interesting point about the possible link between religious and other social divisions, again with very good knowledge and understanding, relevant examples and good analysis.

Another way in which religion can be a source of conflict is when it exists between members of the same religion, where each group claims to have the 'true' meaning of the religion and the way that it should be observed. Examples would be Protestants and Roman Catholics in Northern Ireland, who have a long history of often violent conflict with one another. This again links to Aldridge's point about other divisions, as the political divide is closely bound up with the religious one, with the Unionists (those wishing to remain part of the United Kingdom) being mainly Protestant and the Nationalists (wishing closer involvement with southern Ireland) being mainly Catholics. Other areas of life, particularly education and housing, are also segregated on religious lines. So marked is the segregation that it has been referred to as 'voluntary apartheid'. Despite much legislation attempting to reduce discrimination, the Catholics in Northern Ireland on average suffer greater social deprivation than Protestants.

ⓔ A second way of religion being a source of conflict, again with detailed explanation and analysis of a relevant example.

Another example of this type of 'internal' conflict would be the divisions in Islam between Sunni and Shia Muslims. These share many fundamental beliefs, but also have many differences in rituals, law and theology. While the majority of the world's Muslims are Sunni, making up about 90%, Shia Muslims are in the majority in some countries, including Iran and Iraq. The 1979 Iranian revolution, which resulted in a radical Shia Islamist agenda, led to the invasion by the Sunni Saddam Hussein of Iraq. The resulting war led to the death of some one and half million Muslims, and the social and political consequences are still being felt, not just in those countries but around the world. Here again, though, the conflict was, and remains, as much political as religious.

ℯ **10/10 marks awarded.** A further example, again showing relevant analysis and a breadth of knowledge.

Overall, this is a sophisticated answer, with great attention to detail. Many students would not be able to write this much in the time allowed and the marks could have been gained with less material. It is important to do as many timed answers as possible throughout your course, so that you know roughly how much you can write in the time you allow yourself for each part question.

14 As Item A says, in the last 50 years or so there has been a large growth in the number of New Religious Movements (NRMs), of which sects are a part. However, although different sociologists have attempted to find defining characteristics, there is no single definition of what a sect actually is. The early sects often emerged as part of a schism with the church from which they separated, but this often does not apply to more recent sects.

ℯ A useful start, though it is not made clear whether the lack of definition is actually being offered as a problem of measuring sect membership.

If we assume that we have a working definition of what we could call a sect, one problem of measurement is that many sects had (or have) no formal records of membership. This might be because membership was 'fluid', with people joining and leaving frequently, or because the sect had no formal headquarters where records were stored. This would have been a particular problem before the internet. Another reason why there were no formal records could be that the sect was a secretive, world-rejecting sect whose members had very little, if any, contact with the outside world. This would be the kind of sect referred to in Item A, where many young people, who were often drawn to sects led by charismatic leaders, cut ties with their families. Even larger, better-known sects, such as the Unification Church (Moonies), do not offer any proof of membership. Despite the number of converts attending mass weddings, the claim made by the Unification Church that it has millions of members is thought to be totally false. Although Eileen Barker was able to gain access to the Moonies for her study in the 1980s, she did not find thousands of converts. In fact, it is estimated that in 1976, there were only 150 members of the Unification Church in the UK. So one problem is that many sects have no formal membership lists, and even if they do, might be unwilling to provide them to outsiders and might issue false claims regarding numbers.

e A clearly expressed problem of measuring sect membership, with reference to the Item, a relevant example and some analysis.

> A second problem with measuring sect membership is that there is no list that can be consulted. This is in large part because there is no single accepted definition of what counts as a sect. While some groups, such as Scientologists or Plymouth Brethren, are well known — in the former case, very well known — others only come to public knowledge as a result of a particular action that puts them in the headlines. Examples would be Jim Jones' People's Temple, where some 900 people committed mass suicide, Heaven's Gate, where 37 people took part in a mass suicide, and David Koresh and the Branch Davidians, where over 80 people died in Waco, Texas, following a siege conducted by the FBI. In addition, many sects, especially those with a charismatic leader, are very short-lived, so sect membership would be highly dependent on the point in time that an attempt was made to do a count.

e **9/10 marks awarded.** A second problem identified and discussed, with examples and some brief analysis.

Overall, a good answer using material from the Item, showing understanding of the question and with good use of appropriate examples.

Student B

13 One way in which religion can act as a source of conflict is where some members start what they call a 'Holy War' against others. This is the case with members of Daesh and their Jihadists. People claiming to be from this group have committed several acts of terrorism, many outside their own borders, such as the attacks in Paris in 2015. One result of these attacks is that many people associate them with Islam in general, rather than a particular group, and there has been a wave of anti-Muslim feeling, with some attacks on mosques. This is, of course, not the only example of a Holy War. The Crusades of the eleventh century and onwards were a Holy War fought by Christian knights against Muslims. The Pope promised them forgiveness for their sins if they were able to win back the Holy City of Jerusalem for the Christians. Some religious wars have been fought between members of the same religion, such as those between Catholics and Protestants in France in the sixteenth century.

e An appropriate identification of how religion can cause conflict, with good examples, though it would have been helpful to expand a little on the notion of a 'Holy War'.

> Another source of conflict caused by religion is identified by Marx, who saw religion in terms of one class waging war on another. The ruling class used hegemony to make the working class believe that it was their duty to accept their place in society and that they would be rewarded in heaven.

ⓔ **5/10 marks awarded.** This is very brief and somewhat muddled. Marx did not say that religion caused class conflict — in fact, his view was that it was used to avoid overt conflict, as alluded to in the last sentence. It would have been helpful to explain the concept of hegemony in this context.

Overall, a patchy answer, with the first part much better than the second. In questions where you are asked for two reasons/explanations, etc., try to make the two parts roughly equal, in terms of both the length and the skills displayed.

---

14 Sects are a type of New Religious Movement (NRM) that, as Item A says, grew from the late 1960s.

One problem of measuring membership is that there is no one kind of sect, and some sects are easier to measure than others. A well-established sect such as the Quakers will have proper membership lists as it has a formal organisation and will keep records. Other sects will be so small that they will only have a few members and may operate out of a house or a single church hall, so a sociologist might feel that it is not worth the trouble of trying to get an accurate picture of how many members there are. Some sects are very secretive and would not disclose any details of their membership to outsiders. This would probably be the case with world-rejecting sects, who would be unlikely to allow any non-member to come and ask questions. As it says in the Item, some young people who joined sects cut all ties with their family and friends. There was a moral panic about this, with allegations that some sects were using brain-washing techniques and preventing people from leaving, with the result that some sect leaders became almost paranoid and became even more secretive.

ⓔ A problem of measuring membership is identified and developed, with an example and some analysis. An appropriate reference is made to the Item. It would have been helpful to have given an example of a world-rejecting, or secretive, sect. An interesting point is made about moral panics.

Another problem with measuring sect membership is that there is often no way of checking how accurate the figures are. Some sects claim very large membership figures. The Item says that some claim thousands of members, but Scientology regularly claims that it has some 12 million members worldwide. However, those who have tried to investigate this claim say that the figure appears to have been plucked out of the air, while others say that it in part represents anybody who has ever made an enquiry, bought a book or gone along to any kind of meeting. The consensus appears to be that there are some 30,000 members worldwide — probably less. This is an impressive figure, but far, far less than the number claimed by the organisation. If you are not a secretive sect and are trying to attract members, it will be in your interest to pretend to have more members than you actually do. Measuring the extent of sect membership is impossible, but compared with major religions, the number is very, very small.

e **8/10 marks awarded.** Another problem identified and discussed, with an appropriate example and some analysis.

Overall, a sound answer showing good knowledge and understanding, reference to the Item and analysis.

Practice question

15 Read Item B below and answer the question that follows.

Item B

Many sociologists argue that increasing secularisation is an inevitable feature of modernity. They suggest that the growing acceptance of scientific and rational explanations rather than those based on religious teachings would lead to religious institutions losing their moral authority.

Though data from most Western societies show a fall in the number of those claiming to have a religious faith, others argue that religious adherence may be changing, rather than declining, and that there is still room for the spiritual in modern life.

Applying material from Item B and your own knowledge, evaluate the view that the spread of rational thought and scientific explanations has resulted in a decline in religious faith.

(20 marks)

e There are some important issues to address here, such as the presumed inevitability of secularisation (does the evidence support this?), whether all religious institutions have lost their moral authority, and whether the decline in those professing to have a religious faith is matched by acceptance of scientific and rational explanations.

Knowledge check answers

1 The hypothetico-deductive method.
2 World religions such as Christianity, Islam, Judaism, and some Aboriginal or 'native' religions.
3 Functionalism.
4 Judaism, Sikhism.
5 Taking Holy Communion; Friday prayers at the mosque.
6 An opiate is used to deaden pain, so Marx is suggesting that religion removes or diminishes the pain of exploitation.
7 The outward display of one's wealth, e.g. by driving a top-brand luxury car, wearing designer clothes and expensive jewellery, living in a palatial home.
8 A cross; a crescent; the Star of David.
9 The Pope.
10 Football fans; Goths; 'Trekkies'.
11 Being a priest in the Roman Catholic Church; leading Friday prayers to a mixed congregation in a mosque; being a rabbi in Orthodox Judaism.
12 The status quo is the situation that exists at the moment.
13 Many Christian fundamentalist groups have a presence on the internet and also run radio and television stations, and certain Islamist fundamentalist groups have posted online videos of some of their actions.
14 Certain bishops have seats in the House of Lords.
15 An ideal type is a kind of model of something that draws out its essential characteristics, providing a kind of template against which real examples of the phenomenon can be measured.
16 'Charisma' refers to a quality that is held by powerful personalities that attracts other people to them. A charismatic leader can then attract followers by the strength of his/her personality. Most charismatic leaders of sects are male.
17 Baptists, Lutherans, Plymouth Brethren.
18 It has a mainly middle-class membership; its representatives take part in formal state occasions, e.g. coronations and royal marriages. It is the official religion of England.
19 Most people are innately sociable beings and someone with weak external ties would be likely to welcome the sense of friendship and 'belonging' found in the movement.
20 As the UK is considered a Christian country, many people who did not belong to another religion and who did not feel strongly about declaring that they had 'no religion' would tend to say that they were Christian.
21 They are available only to people who have internet connections. It is very difficult to obtain a representative sample. It is not possible to be sure who is completing the survey.

22 At least partly for demographic reasons — immigrant populations tend to have a younger age profile than the host population. For black people of African origin, there is a strong tradition of evangelical Christianity, so they may be less likely than white populations to be undergoing secularisation in the younger generations.
23 By running retirement homes, making charitable donations to older members, having a system of support workers to help people becoming less able to care for themselves.
24 A weighted sample takes into account the proportion of the units in the sample that are found in the sample as a whole. If, for example, a particular group makes up 2% of your sample but there are actually 6% of such people in the population as a whole, the findings from the 2% will be 'weighted' (given a greater value) so that they represent the actual proportion in the population. Other groups that may be over-represented in the sample will have their values reduced accordingly.
25 This is the first of the three stages that Comte believed that each society experienced. In the theological stage, the causes of natural phenomena are unknown and are therefore attributed to one or several divine or supernatural beings or spirits.
26 This is how individuals are bound together in industrial societies. Social unity is based on interdependence brought about by a complex division of labour, in which people are dependent on each other for the fulfilment of their needs.
27 An atheist believes that there is no god or supernatural being. An agnostic is not sure and therefore has an open mind on the issue. Put simply, an atheist does not believe, while an agnostic does not know.
28 (a) Census forms, official statistics, surveys,
(b) interviews, personal documents, observation (participant or non-participant).
29 Some New Age groups may be so small and/or secretive that few people know of their existence. Many New Age groups have such a loose, informal structure that either there are no 'members' in the formal sense or no membership lists exist.
30 A system of belief which rejects ideas of the supernatural and accepts scientific ideas regarding the nature and origin of natural phenomena, does not believe in an afterlife, suggesting that we give our lives meaning by seeking happiness and helping others to do the same, and believes that ethical and moral decisions should be based on reason and a concern for humans and other living creatures.
31 In the UK, secularisation is thought to be demonstrated by the fall in religious attendance and in those professing religious beliefs, while in the USA, it is suggested that it is the churches themselves that have become more secular.

32 China is a communist society and communism rejects the idea of religion. While there are government-sanctioned religious groups in China, their activities are controlled and religious activities may take place only within registered centres of worship.

33 Gross domestic product. This is the monetary value of all goods and services produced within the borders of a country over a specified period of time, usually a year.

34 The number of births per thousand women of child-bearing age (usually 15–45) in a year.

Index

Note: Page numbers in **bold** indicate defined terms.

Index